To Ella and Phyllis
Friends in Life's Pilgrimage

Through the Eyes of the Saints

A Pilgrimage Through History

Averoldi Polyptych depicting the Resurrection of Christ, the Annunciation,
SS Nazarius and Celsus with Averoldi and the Martyrdom of Sebastian,
1522 (oil on panel)
Titian (Tiziano Vecellio) (c.1488-1576)
Church of Santi Nazaro e Celso, Brescia, Italy
Image courtesy of Bridgeman Art Library
For a discussion of the painting see ch.2, especially pp.13-17.

Through the Eyes of the Saints

A Pilgrimage Through History

David Brown

continuum
LONDON • NEW YORK

Continuum
The Tower Building
11 York Road
London SE1 7NX

15 East 26th Street
New York
NY 10010

www.continuumbooks.com

First published 2005

British Library Cataloguing-in-Publication Data
A catalogue record for this book is available from the British Library.

ISBN 0 8264 7640 6

Typeset by YHT Ltd, London
Printed and bound in Great Britain
by Antony Rowe Ltd, Chippenham, Wilts

Contents

CONTENTS

CONTENTS

Preface

Given the two Greek words from which it comes, 'hagio-graphy' should mean simply writings about the saints, but, as we all know, it has become a term of abuse for cringingly deferential writing that offers nothing but unqualified praise for the individual concerned. It is not surprising, therefore, that, as contemporary scandals make us increasingly aware of the falli-bility of the Church, there has been a corresponding decline in interest in conventional books about the saints. That seems to me a pity because the fault lies in how the saints have been approached, not in the lack of any intrinsic interest to their lives. Approaching them through their fallibility can in fact make them more engaging rather than less, as we discover them struggling with similar dilemmas to our own. One undoubted advantage that the 2000 years of Christian history has over the Scriptures is its ability often to provide much closer parallels to the issues raised by our own lives. This is in no way to imply that the life of Jesus is irrelevant, but it is to acknowledge that it is often easier to think how his example might be applied in quite different circumstances if others have gone before us in trying to work this out in practice.

That is why I have attempted in what follows to achieve two purposes at the same time: both to tell the story of the Church and to draw lessons from the lives of some of the major figures involved. Among professional teachers of theology spiritual issues are not uncommonly contrasted with academic, as though to write about the one is inevitably to abandon standards associated with the other. But there is no necessity that this should be so. Indeed, spiritual insights are likely to be much better grounded, the more thoroughly the lives from which they are derived have been properly investigated and placed in their historical context. That remark may make it sound as though a rather dry academic work now follows. This is not so. The underlying academic apparatus (roughly indicated in the Notes and Further Reading) is kept firmly beneath the surface. Instead, readers are encouraged to focus on the challenges raised by individual lives.

The question of what makes a saint, their present existence in heaven and how they might contribute to our own pursuit of holiness is pursued in the Introduction and Conclusion. However, the main body of the book in the intervening chapters is devoted to tracing major events in the history of the Church through a select number of lives. The choice not only reflects the span of the centuries but also the various branches of the Christian Church. The majority appear in either modern Roman Catholic or Anglican calendars of saints. Some, though, are also included who are listed nowhere. This is to remind the reader how arbitrary such lists can be, not least in respect of certain sorts of individuals. If rulers are one example, married women (seldom recognized) are another.

I have entitled this book *Through the Eyes of the Saints: A Pilgrimage through History* because my aim throughout has been to present the issues these individuals faced as they themselves might have viewed them in their own particular historical context. This is important because we learn most from others when we do not come with predetermined ideas but rather first engage with the world as they saw it. The result, I hope, will be that, for example, there will no longer be a temptation to suppose that saints of the Reformation era (whether Catholic or Protestant) could not possibly transcend the divisions of their age (Cosin, Ferrar and Teresa of Avila all give the lie to any such view). Again, persecutors of heretics can be otherwise good men (Arundel), Cranmer can resist martyrdom for reasons other than cowardice, Wesley achieve great things for God despite and in part because of his poor relations with women, and so on. God continues to speak to us through such people not because they were perfect but precisely because they were so like us in being creatures of their time and circumstance. Where they differed was in trusting God to pull them through into a deeper commitment and holiness.

Introduction

1

The Whole Company of Heaven

Holy imperfection and the medley of difference

Even among Catholic-minded Christians, reading the lives of the saints is a much less popular activity than it used to be. There is a number of reasons for this, some good, some bad. The good include the often saccharine way in which their lives have been recounted, with too much stress on pious devotions and an overscrupulous goodness that is more likely to alienate the modern reader than speak of relevance to their own lives. The adage 'so heavenly minded as to be of no earthly use' is not without point. Equally, the prominence given in those earlier books to an alleged virtue in unquestioning obedience to religious authority, whether Pope or Bible, cannot but strike us today as the surrender of intellect rather than as its creative engagement with life's problems. Whatever faults this book has, they cannot be said to lie along such lines. What attracts me to the saints is precisely their likeness to ourselves in holy *imperfection*, in the way in which their struggle to follow Christ demonstrates their limitations no less than their strengths under divine grace.

Even so, the reader may still be reluctant to follow me in my enthusiasm. So in this introductory chapter, together with the one that follows and a concluding chapter, I want to meet some of the more obvious reservations head-on. The final chapter will examine how the whole notion of heaven and the saints as intercessors might be given more definite and plausible contours. The next chapter tackles the objection that saints somehow undermine the unique role of Christ. In this present chapter, however, I want to explore the question of what purpose might be served by reflection on their lives and in the process indicate why as a consequence I have attempted to offer an outline history of the Church through their lives.

Let me, however, first present the 3practical case against with as much clarity as I can muster. Were it is just a matter of rather too cloying a piety, that would be bad enough, but there is more, much more. For no one can deny that those canonized by the Church are a rum lot. From the fifth century, for instance, comes St Simeon Stylites who spent twenty years on top of a pillar, sixty feet high; from the fourteenth St Catherine of Siena who tried to live on eucharistic wafers alone; from the seventeenth St Margaret Mary Alacoque who scratched Christ's name on her breast. Others tormented themselves in the desert till, not surprisingly, they saw strange visions of the Devil and his entourage − St Antony of Egypt, for one. Then what of those who seem to have got there by mistake, whose morality leaves much to be desired − St Cyril of Alexandria, for example, who used bribery and blackmail to get his way at one of the early Church councils, or St Jerome who, whatever his achievements in creating the Latin version of the Bible, showed scant regard for the truth in blackening his opponents' characters?

And what of all those who never existed? Ursula may possibly have, but certainly not her 11,000 fellow-women massacred at Cologne − 'thousands' only because of a scribal error that mistook the Latin abbreviation M for the numeral (1000) instead of the more plausible 'martyr'. Yet thousands of bones were once on view at Cologne in apparent confirmation of the legend. Or take the once popular story of the female saint known as Wilgefortis on the Continent and as Uncumber in medieval England. According to the legend she refused to marry when her father requested her to do so. Granted a beard by God as a means of warding off unwelcome amorous advances, she faced a wrathful father who took his revenge by having his now bearded daughter crucified. Extraordinary as it may seem, the origin of the legend amounts to no more than the fact that in many early portraits of Christ on the cross he appears bearded and wearing a long tunic (known as a *colobium*). Mistaken for a dress, it was taken to imply the presence of a woman, and the bearded female was then postulated by way of explanation.

It would be all too easy to dismiss such excesses as no more than the folly of a less learned or more gullible age. Yet it is important to note that the Reformation was not necessarily wiser in its day, nor us in ours. So concerned was Cranmer to remove such past follies that his Book of Common Prayer perpetrated others in its turn. Only biblical saints were allowed any major celebration. The result was that until late into the twentieth century, if the medieval calendar of saints resembled a list of the odd and non-existent, the Anglican calendar by contrast looked more like a roll-call of nonentities. For with the exception of Judas Iscariot all the apostles were assigned a central place, yet about most of them we know virtually nothing. Of course preachers continue to make valiant efforts with the like of Philip and James, Bartholomew, Simon and Jude, Matthias, and so on. But I suspect that the resultant homilies are about as near to catching the heart of the individual concerned as were their more learned medieval counterparts in struggling with non-existent saints. So we can only welcome recent attempts on the part of the Anglican Communion to widen its calendar.

Yet ironies remain. A notable instance is the reintroduction of St George as a day for celebrating the Church in England, for, whatever we may think of England, George's story certainly remains as legendary as ever. George, we all know, fought against a dragon to save a lady in distress. Less familiar now is the dragon in the story of St Margaret of Antioch. According to her legend the Devil, disguised as a dragon, tried to swallow her only to find himself forced to disgorge his prey:

Margaret successfully used the cross about her neck to force him to cough her up. Both accounts may sound like romantic nonsense, but it is important to note the serious meat in Margaret's legend, for it indicates the lengths people were prepared to go to find models for their experience, when the Church itself failed to provide them in actual living exemplars. That struggle with a dragon was taken to symbolize women in general struggling in pregnancy to give birth, and so Margaret became one of the most popular saints of the Middle Ages as patroness of childbirth. Not a particularly complimentary image for the process, one may observe, but it did offer a sturdy realism that reflected the high proportion of women who once died in childbirth (and indeed still do in less developed societies). In a Church reluctant to canonize married women, myth had to take over, and so women found in the legendary Margaret someone with whom they could identify.

Catherine of Alexandria is a similar case in point. The story went that in defending her faith she had defeated in debate no less than fifty pagan philosophers before being thrown to be tortured onto her infamous wheel (from which the Catherine-wheel of modern firework displays derives its name). All those philosophers were men, and so her legend once more gave a handle for reflection and example where real life fell short: an educated woman who was not a nun displaying wisdom and intelligence. Little wonder then that when, in the fourteenth century, Catherine of Siena sought to reform the medieval papacy, she took the other Catherine as one of her own models, just as in due course Josephine Butler was in the nineteenth century to use Catherine of Siena as her own exemplar in her fight for women's rights.

But it was not just in the struggles of childbirth and for education that the two fictitious saints gave inspiration. They commanded wider respect as general precedents for women taking initiative, as a more familiar saint well illustrates: for along with St Michael the Archangel it was to Catherine and Margaret that Joan of Arc appealed in her campaign to liberate France. Joan broke so many norms – dressing in male clothing, fighting as a warrior, reprimanding prince and cleric alike – that it is perhaps not surprising that it took 500 years before she was formally canonized. Burnt at the stake under English pressure in 1431, she was not declared a saint until 1920. But even today at the start of the third millennium, with a pope who has canonized more individuals than all his predecessors, the great majority of those being canonized by the papacy remain men, and clergy and nuns still far outnumber laity. Yet the reality, we all know, is not like that; sanctity is just as common among laity as clergy. Indeed, given that there are so many more lay members of the Church than clerical, this of itself should have generated a larger number formally recognized but it has not. Just occasionally, the medieval world saw the problem. St Margaret of Scotland (d. 1093) was someone who rolled Margaret and Catherine into one, as it were. Both wife and educated, she was in fact the mother of eight children and someone who could read – unlike her illiterate husband, Malcolm III. Yet the sad truth is that her elevation owed more to her royal status than to these qualities, just as St Louis of France (d. 1270) was unlikely, as being both a warrior and married, ever to have been canonized, had it not been for his position as King of France as Louis IX.

So one cannot deny that much is wrong with this history, and that the presence or absence of the title 'saint' remained to some degree arbitrary, even after the process had been formalized at the end of the twelfth century. That is one reason why I feel fully justified in what follows in making my selection not only from the lists of more than one denomination but also sometimes even well beyond that. But the spread is deliberate for another reason. All of us are conscious of the accelerating speed of change. If the America and Europe of 1900 were hugely different from what they were like in 1800, this is even more true of the contrast between 2000 and 1900. That makes it all the more imperative that there are bridges to help span the gap between the nature of the summons to holiness in the Palestine of Christ's day and in our own hugely different world.

It is all very well to say all that matters is that Christians should seek to follow the example of their Lord, but, given how different circumstances often are from those of his day, this becomes no easy task to work out in practice. Jesus, for example, lived a life bereft of earthly power, and so once Christians came to such power those in positions of responsibility had a difficult task in translating his way of acting into their own lives. Similarly, unless pacifism was to be deemed the right course under all circumstances, it was a hard task for the Christian soldier to think through what it might mean to act in a Christ-like way as a soldier. Again, Jesus was both male and unmarried, and so women often had to do intellectual somersaults (as with Margaret of Antioch) in order to think through what a vocation to holiness might mean in their own very different station in life.

All the examples so far mentioned might raise themselves in almost any age, whereas others come to greater prominence in one century rather than another. How is evangelism to be conducted among pagans? If state and Church are alike part of the providence of God, what is one to do when their interests conflict? How much deference should be shown to those in authority in the Church? In a divided Church, are examples always to be sought exclusively from those of similar belief to oneself? Are slavery or colonialism secondary issues or integral to how one practises the gospel? How should Christians view their Jewish inheritance in a post-Holocaust world? The questions flood in. One could of course approach all these kinds of issue in purely theoretical terms: but looking at how others in the past have in practice approached such problems will, I believe, bring a measure of realism to whatever conclusions we draw. In particular, it will chasten modern arrogance that contemporary insights are enough, and that there is no need to learn from the experience of past generations.

As I have suggested elsewhere, temporal, spatial and metaphysical distance between us and Christ can all be greatly reduced by close attention to such past lives.[1] By metaphysical distance I mean the fact that, however human Christ was (and he was of course fully human), it is still a humanity that stands at a considerable distance from our own, in its perfection and in its closeness to his Father and ours. So in some ways it is easier to explore our dilemmas more indirectly through what imperfect followers have done, people like us who have not always made the right decisions or been confident that what they do is really in accord with the divine will. But there is also the question of temporal and spatial distance. Palestine 2000 years ago bore little resemblance to medieval Rome, far less modern Britain. So anything that can bring us just a little bit closer to what it might mean to lead a Christ-like life in our world is surely to be welcomed.

In what follows, therefore, I have deliberately focused on elements in the saints' lives that might illumine our present. Many of the principal moments in the Church's developing history are identified as these stories are told, but on each occasion my primary aim has been to locate what lessons they might have to teach us today. Trying to establish both historical context and contemporary relevance may sound like incompatible aims, but my point is simply that we need to appreciate difference before we can assimilate similarities. Change has always been with us, but it is only if we recognize this fully that we will benefit from it. History teaches us, for example, that Gregory the Great made possible the modern authoritarian papacy; his own life suggests that he had a quite different and better model in mind. Catherine of Siena was a creature of her time in the extremities of asceticism to which she felt called, but it may have been that same asceticism that gave her the necessary confidence to reprimand even popes. And so on.

The terms 'Reformation' and 'Renaissance' alike suggest a return to earlier norms – putting the faith back in its old form, bringing classical values to life again. But in neither case was that exactly what happened. So far, however, from this being a weakness, it was a strength precisely because, while the old can refresh, taken just as it was it will become simply a straitjacket. Indeed, the old will be forced in any case into new ways, as it struggles to develop relevance to its new setting. That is one reason why legends of saints were constantly being rewritten, as martyrs of distant times such as Margaret of Antioch and Catherine of Alexandria were made to offer new lessons. As a young adult I well remember being deeply impressed when the local parish priest introduced the Sanctus by stressing the last phrase in the words 'with angels, and archangels, and the whole company of heaven'. It was his way of gathering into our worship all the faithful dead. Cranmer, however, had intended no such thing. The original Latin which he was translating had clearly meant the heavenly host, angelic contingents as it were. But the priest's error was a happy one. It reminds us that renewal comes from looking at the old in new ways. There are huge differences between the individuals discussed in the pages that follow, but it is that very medley of difference that forms, I believe, the source of their strength. Each of us can find our own characteristic problem addressed by one or other of them.

But is this perhaps to put too much weight on others and not enough on Christ? Is the significance of the incarnation thereby undermined? It is to this objection that I next turn.

2

Christ and his Train

The bishop and the artist

Why should Easter matter? Christ may break forth from the tomb, but if this is a unique exception reserved for God's Son, marvellous though that is, ultimately it can say little to the rest of us. Christianity of course from the first has asserted quite the contrary. Jesus is 'the first fruits of the dead', Paul tells us (1 Cor. 15.20), while elsewhere he speaks of the ascension in terms of Christ leading a host of released captives in his train (cf. Eph. 4.8). Even so, that relation between him and us can be portrayed in more than one way – as close or distant, as proceeding in only one direction or as interactive and interdependent. In order to explore how best the relationship might be conceived, it will be helpful to explore how it has been treated in the history of art. As will emerge in due course, the presence or absence of saints can play a crucial role.

Modern readings of the Apostles' Creed tend to take the clause that refers to Christ's descent into hell as a way of alluding to his plummeting to the very depths of human suffering on the cross. The more ancient understanding, however, was quite different. The phrase was taken as our primary clue to the meaning of Easter, and given a strong inclusive reference. Christ has burst the gates of hell (meaning here a place of waiting and not of punishment) and all the faithful dead now join with him in his victory. Indeed, for the Eastern Orthodox this remains their principal icon of the resurrection, and so

11

instead of the western image of Christ standing alone on his tomb that descent forms the principal visual focus for their Easter celebrations. Christ stands triumphant on the broken doors of hell, but not alone, as he pulls the dead up to join him, among them Adam and Eve and also many of the other leading figures of the Old Testament, including David and Solomon, recognizable by their crowns.

Initial reflection might suggest that the modern western image must have the edge, since here realism replaces myth and a serious attempt is made to portray how Christ might have re-emerged from the tomb. After all, it may be said, it all sounds faintly comic to suppose that Christ stepped down from his cross, as it were, and then travelled to some nether region where the release of the dead was made effectual before he returned once more to earth to appear to his disciples. If the icon is taken literally, that of course must inevitably seem to be so. But that something symbolic might be the real meaning appears indicated already as early as the New Testament itself, where Matthew has the dead coming out of their tombs as Christ is crucified (Mt. 27.53). Matthew can scarcely have meant this literally; otherwise what happened to those resuscitated corpses? Rather, it is his way of recording the fact that Christ's death (and thus also his resurrection) has an immediate impact for others. His work is not for himself alone, he does not rise alone, but brings numerous others in his train.

Put in that wider context, it is now the western image that seems the less appealing. Christ emerging from the tomb stands as an isolated individual, a unique exception that, so far at least as the paintings under review are concerned, gives no clue as to what potential relevance the event might have for us. One might of course turn to the Scriptures themselves for the answer, but these in turn raise further problems for the image. For the western form fails to take seriously the reticence of the evangelists shown in their omitting to recount the actual moment of resurrection. No doubt that was one reason why for many centuries such presentations were also resisted in the west: they were felt to pry too much into something essentially other, and so to denude the event of its essential mystery. Certainly, most images of Christ stepping on his sarcophagus seem strangely pedestrian, even those from otherwise great artists such as Giotto. Even with asleep or puzzled soldiers at Christ's feet, there is little to evoke wonder or awe.

It was clearly a difficulty with which some Renaissance artists wrestled, as various experiments were made with more dramatic options. Michelangelo, for instance, tries to play on the physical power of Christ's strong, youthful body to conjure up the notion of death defeated.[2] More commonly, however, the pattern employed was to borrow imagery from the ascension and portray Christ shooting out of his tomb heavenwards. It is one such image (from Titian) that Tom Wright uses for the front cover of his impressive recent lengthy work on the resurrection, The Resurrection of the Son of God, in which he is concerned to stress the physical reality of Christ's resurrection.[3] I would not wish to quarrel with that emphasis, but his choice of illustration does raise acutely this question of the precise relationship between Christ's survival of death and our own. The image chosen is in fact only the central panel of what is a polyptych, an altarpiece from Brescia in northern Italy where a number of subsidiary paintings are intended to complement and inform our reading of the central illustration.[4] By isolating one element a quite different meaning from that intended by Titian is in fact generated. All the focus now falls on Christ as an isolated individual, whereas Titian deliberately includes others, notably saints. Why that is a difference of no small moment can best be indicated by considering the different underlying theologies that motivate artist and theologian.

Not long after writing Resurrection, Tom Wright not only became a diocesan bishop but also produced another much shorter work that nicely illustrates this dispute and is of particular relevance to the topic of this book. In For All The Saints? the theme of the familiar hymn is deliberately called into question by the title's question mark.[5] Any attempt to pick out particular individuals and celebrate their lives detracts, he believes, from the unique significance of Christ and what he has done for us. Instead, what he wants is a return to what he sees as the biblical view, a hope that looks to the end of history and the resurrection of our bodies in that distant time. In his view the Church is wrong to speak of growth in the meantime in another world (sometimes called purgatory), and still more misguided in speaking of key holy figures, the saints, as already with Christ in heaven and interceding on our behalf. For Wright this undermines the radical egalitarianism of the New Testament which treats us all as saints, as the holy people of God, reduces the role of the new life as wholly a divine gift, and distorts the focus of Christian expectation, that everything is working towards a single great hope, the consummation of all things at the end of history. As you might expect from a distinguished New Testament scholar, this is argued with frequent appeal to New Testament texts. But there is also some use of parody. He speaks of belief in a place of growth and purgation as rather like supposing most of us to be dirty country yokels who need a good scrubbing before we can be admitted to the heavenly court, while the idea of saints already in heaven, he tells us, is rather like friends at the palace, whom we hope will put in a good word for us, for we certainly cannot do it for ourselves.[6] The parody is not without its element of truth, but distortions should not be allowed to disguise from us the real heart of the doctrine.

To see what that heart is we need once more to return to Titian's painting and to the work as a whole. In the other panels one finds at the upper level the angel Gabriel with Mary, and lower down on one side St Sebastian and on the other, alongside the donor, the saints to whom the Brescian church was dedicated, Saints Nazarius and Celsus. Within church circles the Renaissance is often blamed for too much individualism. Ironically, however, it seems to me that it is Tom Wright who illustrates the modern fault rather than Titian. For consider why Titian has included these additional elements. Superficially, a response might be given in terms of the wishes of his patron, the papal legate Altobello Averoldi. But at a deeper level one must go on to ask whether there was anything in church teaching that might have induced patron and artist alike to opt for the more complex pattern, and the answer surely is that there was. The inclusion of a reference to the annunciation emphasizes that it was Mary's 'yes' to the angel that made Jesus' life and thus the resurrection ultimately possible. Equally, that the resurrection continues to have an impact is due in no small measure to the example of the saints who followed in Christ's footsteps. In other words, Christ does not act alone; he was shaped by the communion of saints, most obviously by Mary his mother, and he continues to act through holy men and women.

Of course, God can do anything, and so such human mediation might have been avoided, but the message of the incarnation is that it was not. God entering fully into our humanity meant allowing himself to become dependent on others both in his earthly life and subsequently. Think of those thirty or so years on earth. For Jesus to be truly human, like us he would need to learn as does any other child, and so be dependent not only on education in his home but also no less from people of whom the gospels have left little or no record, such as the local rabbi. Equally, in expounding his message of love his understanding would have been shaped not only through his prayers but also by ordinary human relationships such as those with his mother and family and with his female and male disciples. Nor should we hesitate to find in others possible sources of his teaching. Its distinctiveness is hardly abrogated by its initial stimulus coming from elsewhere. So, for instance, John the Baptist may well have been responsible for the urgency of Jesus' summons to repentance, but there is nonetheless a harshness to John's preaching that Jesus' lacks (e.g. Mt. 3.11–12). Again, it is not impossible that it was his exchange with the Syro-Phoenician woman (Mk 7.24–30) that led him to give a higher status to Gentiles in the divine economy than seems to have been true generally among his contemporaries. Certainly, all agree that it is an odd exchange, and so may possibly have been preserved precisely because the woman's quick response led Jesus to think anew: his compatriots' abusive term for Gentiles as like the despised wild dogs of the day just would not do. None of this can be proved, but, the more seriously we take New Testament scholarship's contextualizing of Jesus' teaching within the thought forms of the time, the more likely such scenarios become.

But the same is no less true for the generations that follow. Intriguingly, although one of the most familiar passages in Paul urges imitation of Christ (Phil. 2.5–11), in many other passages it is to his own example that he appeals (e.g. 1 Cor. 7.8, Gal. 4.12). In so doing he was not being arrogant but recognizing an immediacy that was not always available in the case of Christ himself. Readers will be well aware of the extent to which their own faith has been formed and aided by others. Perhaps more commonly this will have been through personal contact, but sometimes it will also have been through what they have heard or read, and it is here that the saints come into their own. Titian's choice of saints is not the easiest to comprehend, but nonetheless they can be used to illustrate that sense of continuing dependency. Sebastian was martyred at the beginning of the fourth century under the Emperor Diocletian (d. 313), and the same may also possibly be true of Nazarius and Celsus, although legend placed their martyrdom considerably earlier, under the Emperor Nero (d. 68). What launched the desire for a fuller story was the discovery of their bones in 395 in a garden outside Milan by its then bishop, Ambrose. Sebastian's story too is largely legend. But amid all the elaboration, we should not miss the deeper motivation for the inclusion of the three saints in a polyptych such as this.

Brescia was a mere fifty-two miles from Milan, and so the presence of Nazarius and Celsus helped bridge the distance from more customary sites of martyrdom such as Palestine or Rome. Sanctity, we are being told, was possible close-by, and not just in far distant centres of power or influence. Admittedly, Rome was where Sebastian was supposedly martyred, but the reason for his inclusion here has really nothing to do with martyrdom at all. Sixteenth-century Italy was still subject to plague, and along with St Roche Sebastian was one of the saints to whom appeal was customarily made in such distress. The reason was twofold: the plague was called the arrow of death, and Sebastian had been killed by arrows; then, the marks caused by an arrow on the body, especially when the attempt was made to remove it, were often not unlike the boils that came with the plague. Of course, one cannot but regret the appeal to myth rather than historical precedent, but the recourse was one of desperation. The Church had failed to authorize models in more closely analogous circumstances. So Sebastian had to be used instead to provide an example of how to face death well in the agonizing circumstances of the plague.

But was the use of such examples not potentially dangerous, distorting rather than deepening Christian faith? Is Tom Wright perhaps after all right that the saints were treated in effect as friends at court, as intercessors with God, and so thereby robbed Christ of his central significance? That this sometimes happened cannot, I think, be denied. Even so, this was not the main point. The problem was that the more exalted a position Christ was given, the more unique his form of life and intimacy with the Father claimed to be, the more problematic following his example became. People needed to see how translation was to be made into their own lives, and just as Paul tried to help by offering his own life, so did the saints of subsequent generations.

Presenting Christ as entirely autonomous and self-sufficient is therefore quite the wrong track to pursue. It is not true in any case to the most likely facts of Jesus' own earthly experience. But, even if it were true, such a being could offer little help to individuals in situations quite different then from Christ's own, for again and again what we find is the necessity of depending on others in order to achieve our goals. Dependence is then for me the right conclusion to draw: dependence for Christ both in his earthly life and in the mediation of what this life might mean in the often very different circumstances of subsequent generations. If I am anywhere near right in all of this, radical consequences then follow in terms of how the Church now functions as a community. Contemporary theology, it seems to me, is often at its most arrogant in claiming that unlike contemporary society and its politicians it has a strong doctrine and practice of social interdependence. Indeed, appeal to the notion of God as Trinity is now almost a commonplace in justifying such a view. Personally, I am much less confident that this is so. So keen are theologians to assert our absolute dependence on Christ for all aspects of salvation that, whatever may be said about relations within the godhead, a strongly independent Christ soon re-emerges as the model for relations within the Church, with essentially a top-down view as the paradigm of how things ought to be. The papacy is an obvious case in point, but bishops in the Anglican Communion are often not far behind: the contemporary Church of England seems to have adopted wholesale what in terms of the history of the Church has been only one possible model for episcopacy, the view that sees this as the ministry most directly derived from Christ, with ordinary priesthood and lay ministry then essentially derivative and wholly dependent on the bishop for its validity. The parish priest becomes treated as a mere surrogate for the bishop, who is viewed as properly the president at each eucharist. The modern practice of bishops summoning their clergy to be present on the very day our Lord instituted the sacrament (Maundy Thursday) also seems to entail such a view – from Christ through the bishop to the priest and then to the people.

But why believe all of this? Paul in talking of Christ as head of the body and us as its limbs already implicitly concedes the indispensability of the limbs to the head no less than of the head to the limbs (Col. 1.18; 2.19; cf. 1 Cor. 12.12–26). Indeed, he goes so far as to talk of 'in his own flesh completing what is lacking in Christ's afflictions for the sake of the body, that is the church' (Col. 1.24). Dependency, therefore, needs today to be rethought in a multiplicity of ways, to develop a fully collaborative understanding of what it means for the Church to be Christ's body in our own day: with dependence flowing, as it were, as much from Christ as to him.

In some of the lives surveyed in the chapters that follow interdependency will be very much to the fore. In others, though saints, the individuals concerned will prove to be no less authoritarian than their less holy contemporaries. But either way, what matters is how both types of saint witness alike to our understanding of the gospel message deepened by their lives, with them not simply as imitators of a single, simple model but Christ mediated through them by that example applied in new circumstances and ages. Christ knew such interdependency in his own life, and knows it still as exalted Lord. Easter will only truly become a joyous reality for us all when we too acknowledge such a mutual interchange.

Part I: The Early Church

3

Polycarp and Perpetua

Martyrdoms real and not so real

Everyone knows that February 14th is St Valentine's Day; very many fewer, who he was; perhaps no one, how the link with love was first established. On that last point one theory is that this was a way of marking when birds were first seen to pair. As for who he was, here too there is some doubt, but almost certainly his widespread veneration was the result of a confusion between two different people. One was a third-century martyr from Terni about seventy miles north-east of Rome (about whom we know virtually nothing) who was the founder of an important church on the Flaminian Way in Rome itself. The prestige of that church was such that it generated a detailed story about its founder. In similar fashion another famous church in Rome, this time in the Trastevere quarter, was also eventually to win canonization for its founder. The cult of St Cecilia, patron saint of music, like that of Valentine, was thus largely a product of fiction, a fine story of martyrdom but mainly fiction nonetheless.

That helps explains why, although Valentine and Cecilia both find a place in commemorations in the 1662 Book of Common Prayer as well as in the Roman Missal, in our more historically conscious age both are either demoted or else disappear altogether (as was the case in the 1980 Anglican Alternative Service Book). But what it does not explain is why there should have been a temptation to produce such fictions in the first place and on such a large scale. It is this question which I want to confront, to discover what the answer might teach us about the potential impact of Christ's life and death on our own. There is both a good side and a bad to be observed which I will illustrate in a moment through some actual early martyrdoms, but first, let me alert the reader to the extent of invented stories in this context, for they too can teach us something about our faith.

In the Introduction I have already alluded to the stories of St Catherine of Alexandria, St Margaret of Antioch and St George, all three popular choices for a church's dedication in the Middle Ages. In all probability they either never existed or else did so in a form far distant from how we now know them. Yet, even when the bare fact of martyrdom is known for certain, this has often been elaborated into a rich, if implausible, legend. Take St Lawrence. A third-century deacon of the church in Rome, he may well, as the story goes, have presented the poor in his community when the treasures of the church were demanded of him; but it is very much a later development that tells us of his torture on the famous gridiron – as is the elaboration of the life of another historical third-century martyr, Agatha, whose severed breasts, we are told, were presented on a plate.

This lust for martyrdom, and for elaborate versions of it at that, eventually became projected back into the New Testament itself. For soon even the apostles themselves were no longer regarded as respectable unless an appropriate martyrdom could be credited to them; hence the reason why even to this day red stoles (the sign of blood) are worn on their feast days. The legend of Bartholomew, for example, is that he was flayed alive, which is why he is usually represented in art with a knife in his hand or else somewhere in the background. Matthew gets an axe, because he is supposed to have been beheaded; St Jude, a lance or halberd, and so the list might go on. Even St John, whom Scripture implies was allowed to live to a ripe old age (Jn 21.17–23), was still provided with the next best thing; two attempts on his life, from both of which he miraculously escaped: a poisoned cup, in which the poison turned into a snake and slithered away, and a cauldron of burning oil, from which he jumped out unhurt.

Although keeping these stories alive is essential if the meaning behind much art and stained glass is not to be lost, my concern here is not historical or artistic. It is to emphasize how important the cult of the martyrs remained, even after Christianity ceased to be a persecuted religion in the fourth century. People just could not get enough of such stories, and so fresh ones had to be invented. But why? What lay behind the need?

At a trivial level one might give the answer that every society needs its heroes, and the martyrs were certainly that. Christianity would probably have survived without them, as persecution under the Roman Empire was spasmodic and erratic: the emperors Decius (d. 251) and Diocletian (d. 313) were by no means the norm. Even so, it might then have survived only in a weaker, less vibrant form. That the challenge of paganism was met head on and defeated was due in no small part to the courage of those prepared to die for their faith, rather than worship the emperor or offer some other sign of loyalty to the existing status quo. To their pagan contemporaries – and one suspects also to some of their fellow Christians – they seemed like fanatics, worrying needlessly about some token burning of incense before a statue of the emperor (the required submission). But what in effect they were fighting for was the distinctiveness, the uniqueness of Christianity, and that they preserved. Yet there was also a downside. For there seems little doubt that martyrdoms were valued in part because they were seen as a very literal following of the example of Christ, the offering of the sacrifice of one's life just as he had done. It was not only that the theology was wrong (our flawed offering cannot be compared with Christ's) but there was also the failure to appreciate that imitating Christ does not require identical but analogous behaviour, whatever is best suited in one's own particular situation, which may be quite different.

But there is more to be said than this. Two other factors also played their part, both more directly relevant to our own world and each well illustrated by the two earliest detailed accounts of martyrdom that we now possess, almost certainly contemporary with the events themselves. One is that of Polycarp, who was martyred at Smyrna (modern Izmir in present-day Turkey) around the middle of the second century, and the other of Perpetua, martyred in 203 at Carthage in north Africa. At one level they could scarcely be more different. Polycarp had known St John the Evangelist as a young man, but was now a bishop in his eighty-sixth year; Perpetua was a young woman who had recently given birth and whose maid, Felicitas, also gives birth while they await their sentence in prison. Perpetua's account is written partly in her own words; Polycarp's by the hand of an admiring follower. But, despite the differences of location, age and ecclesial position, a strong sense of shared vision of what martyrdom is all about clearly emerges.

The first feature of this vision is the conviction that identification with Christ can transform our lives, including even those things of which we are most afraid: suffering and death. And there we now have a more positive clue to why the martyrs were seen as so important by subsequent generations. For they gave the good news to the Church that it was not just Christ who triumphed over suffering and death, but that we all could do likewise. So, significantly, the account of Polycarp's death opens by describing it as 'another divine manifestation of the martyrdom which we read in the gospels', in other words Jesus' passion and death.[7] Then Polycarp deliberately goes to his death in a literal following of Christ's example – riding on an ass. When he gets there, he is tied to the stake 'like a noble ram', in other words like the sacrificial Lamb whom he is following, only to find that the flames have no effect on him, such is his confidence in Christ. Likewise, Perpetua's story opens by remarking that 'instances of ancient faith' need fresh illustration in the immediate present, and thereafter we are taken through the story of how the two young women were able without trembling to face what we all normally fear, such was their confidence in Christ. Their last act is the exchange of the kiss of peace, before they are savaged to death by a mad cow.

Already in both accounts there is the tendency towards the miraculous that would become such a prominent feature of later versions. Polycarp, we are told, had to be dispatched with a dagger because the flames had no effect; while of Perpetua it is remarked that 'so great a woman ... could not have been slain had she not herself willed it'.[8] Later accounts of martyrdom such as Catherine's or Margaret's will speak of half a dozen attempts at the body's destruction before final success. But to smile or laugh at this would be a big mistake. For what we have is a pictorial way of emphasizing a profound and perennial Christian truth: that all that we most fear, in particular suffering and death itself, can indeed be overcome in Christ.

There is also a second key element that these two martyrdoms share. Both writers are convinced that martyrdom brings benefit not only to the person that endures it but also to the entire Christian community. In the case of Perpetua, as she lies languishing in prison, she has a number of visions. In one vision she reconciles her priest and bishop, who had quarrelled and departed this life unreconciled. Two concern her brother, Dinocrates, who had died of cancer of the face at the age of seven. In the first she sees him struggling unsuccessfully to obtain some water from a vast vat, too high for him to reach, the wound on his face still gaping and sore. Her response is to launch into days of prayer for him, at the end of which she has a second vision, this time of his wound healed and of him not only obtaining water to drink but happily splashing about in the vat, as any seven-year-old well might. Her prayers and suffering, the second vision tells her, have transformed that face and given him new life.

Polycarp's martyrdom offers no such dramatic incidents. Nonetheless there are clear parallels. Thus in describing the fire encircling the body, the author declares that it was 'not like a human being in flames but like a loaf baking in the oven'. The last words that Polycarp says leave us in no doubt that a eucharistic reference is intended by this analogy. For those words seem modelled on what he might have said in his church at the eucharist, as there was as yet no set formula. He prays:

'May I be received into your presence this day as a sacrifice right and acceptable, even as you did appoint and foreshadow.' His death has become an extension of Christ's death; like it, an offering – the loaf – that brings nourishment to others.

So used are we to thinking of our faith in highly individualistic terms that such language draws us up sharply. But were not Polycarp and Perpetua right: that not only can Christ transform our fears, he can also work through us as his body to bring healing and reconciliation both in this life and the next? As Christians we are part of the one community of the living and the dead, and so what we offer, what we pray for in Christ, has the power to bring about new life both in this world and the world to come.

Sadly, it is a message that later commentators were often reluctant to endorse, especially when it seemed to envisage a wideness in divine mercy that extended well beyond the borders of the Christian community. So, although Augustine of Hippo preached at least three sermons on Perpetua as his fellow north-African, he insists that her brother must have been baptized for the change to have occurred. What he finds shocking and just cannot come to terms with is that she could have prayed for a now dead non-Christian, still less that her prayers were effective in securing his healing and happiness in that other world, but there is no doubt that that is what Perpetua's text means. In similar vein to Augustine, the medieval reference book known as *The Golden Legend* has her summarily dismiss her relations, 'Get away from me, you enemies of God, for I do not know you,' and she is even made to hurl her infant son to the ground as demonstration of the fact that nothing matters in comparison to her readiness for martyrdom.[9] By contrast, her own version of events speaks of her concern that the child should be entrusted to the care of her own immediate family.

'Martyr' in Greek literally means 'witness'. Our ancestors in the faith usurped the word to speak uniquely of those who patterned their death after that of Christ. Even then, though, it can speak of witness to two quite different realities: to trust in

God and in the breadth of his love or to a narrow sectarianism and exclusiveness that thinks literal imitation enough. The challenge to us today is to appropriate what is best in those early accounts, whether legendary or actual. Then we will find in Christ our fears destroyed and suffering and death not the final victors, but instead a communion of living and dead in Christ, all being healed and restored through the present, active power of that living Lord.

4

Antony of Egypt

The desert blossoming in rural Scotland

A visit to the Monks' Dormitory in the Cloisters of Durham Cathedral will reveal an impressive array of Anglo-Saxon sculptured crosses, many copies from elsewhere. The tallest and most elaborately carved is the Ruthwell Cross, the original of which, dating from the late seventh century, now stands inside the parish church at Ruthwell in rural Galloway in south-west Scotland. Its carvings include one of Christ standing in triumph over two animals. The accompanying Latin inscription declares: 'Beasts and dragons recognized in the desert the saviour of the world.' Immediately beneath is another carving that takes up a related theme. Its inscription informs us that what we have is two men breaking bread together 'in the desert'. One of them, Paul, is a rather shadowy figure, about whom we know little. But it is quite otherwise with the other man, Antony. A native Egyptian, whose first and only language was Coptic, he died three centuries before the creation of the Ruthwell Cross, in 356. But why make an Egyptian so central to the exposition of Christianity in far-off Scotland? And why no less than two references to the desert – in the very midst of all that rich farmland of Galloway?

To understand why, and what the connexion is with the Ruthwell Cross, we need to start with a question that may seem to admit of an obvious answer, and that is what is meant by the term 'desert'. Most of us, I suspect, think of the Sahara, with miles upon miles of sand, and nothing living to be seen anywhere. But the biblical deserts of Palestine and Sinai are rather different. When rain falls in March and April, the desert there does indeed 'blossom abundantly' (Isa. 35.2). Not only that, in biblical times such places were alive with wild animals – gazelles and ostriches, wolves and foxes, hyenas and leopards. Deserts were thus most certainly arid places, but also potentially alive, potentially bursting with the possibilities of new life and new hope. Yet at the same time they were also threatening, with no guarantee of water to slake one's thirst and no human habitation nearby as a quick refuge when a pack of wild animals loomed on the horizon.

It is that ambiguity upon which the Bible plays, and which makes the notion of the desert such a rich one within the Christian tradition. Jesus himself has to face the desert before his ministry can begin (Matt. 4.1). There 'in the wilderness' he confronts demons – threatening alternatives to his vocation – and defeats them. In placing Jesus' struggle with temptation in the desert, almost certainly the evangelists intended not just such negative allusions but also the positive side of the image, the blossoming desert. For it was in the desert at Sinai that Israel's primary experience of God had been located, and it is a recurring theme of the prophets that it is in the wilderness that Israel will come to know God once more (e.g. Hos. 2.14–16).

Mark even plays havoc with geography to make the point, though this is concealed from us by most modern translations. From chapter 6 we learn that the miracle of the feeding of the 5000 took place near Bethsaida (v. 45) in what the Authorized Version rightly translates as 'a desert place', but which is now most commonly rendered as 'a lonely place' (e.g. RSV, NEB, JB). What has made our contemporaries twitchy is that there are no deserts in Bethsaida; it is part of verdant Galilee. But it is really Mark's way of telling us that with Christ the desert will blossom once more; as with the feeding of the 5000, new life will emerge, with God in our midst.

Now jump three centuries. In 313 the Emperor Constantine's Edict of Milan marked the beginning of imperial favour for

Christianity, while 325 saw the emperor himself presiding over the first universal council of the Church at Nicaea, near the new imperial capital of Constantinople (modern Istanbul). It looked as though Christianity was now about to settle for a comfortable relation with the society within which it was set. Yet from only the immediately preceding year (324) comes our earliest reference to a monk – on an Egyptian papyrus, while 313 was the very year in which Antony reputedly withdrew to his 'interior desert' near the Red Sea. Monasticism as retreat to the desert was beginning precisely at the point at which Christianity in its other forms was taking control of society.

The coincidence is not accidental. Martyrdom was the old, more obvious form of rebellion against society's values; monasticism, retreat to the desert, the new. And it began like Christ with a decision to face one's own personal demons, before one could be of any help to others. 'Monk' comes from a Greek word (*monachos*) which means 'alone', and it was as the life of a solitary that monasticism began with Antony's retreat. His local bishop, Athanasius, wrote a life of him in which the mythological presentation is to the fore, but if one finds that too much, seven of Antony's letters also survive, and these are full of good, common sense, in particular the recurring theme that all knowledge must start with understanding oneself. 'He who knows himself, knows all men', Antony declares, and it was from that basic insight that he was able to help the constant stream of visitors who came to seek his advice. It was also that same insight that enabled the desert eventually to flower, as one of his successors, Pachomius, turned monasticism into a community ideal. Having all things in common became possible because each of the monks had faced what in themselves led to envy and possessiveness. The desert had at last become the alternative city. Much later, Jerome is the first to tell the story of Paul and Antony sharing a loaf. Even if untrue, the tale has at least this much in its favour, that it indicates how Antony prepared the way for an alternative, more communitarian ideal.

And there we connect at last once more with the Ruthwell Cross. As in Columba's flight from Ireland to Iona, Celtic monasticism insisted upon retreat to the desert. The monastery was there as a standing critique of the society in which it was set. A more establishment model was, however, on its way, with the defeat of Celtic Christianity at the Synod of Whitby in 664. It is intriguing, therefore, to observe that a very similar cross at Bewcastle, much nearer the new centres of power (such as Wilfred's Hexham), omits not only all reference to the desert but any portrayal at all of Antony. The desert has now become an embarrassment, instead of a challenge.

The history of monasticism thereafter is the story of continuing embarrassment alternating with one reforming movement succeeding another, as initial enthusiasm wanes. The desert that can blossom, that alternative city, is certainly no easy vision, but the great strength of monasticism at its best has always been the standing critique it has been able to offer of whatever society it finds itself in. Today as a movement it is weak, but that is not because there is anything problematic with its ideals. The need to share and transcend selfishness remains as basic as ever. Today's problem is surely more basic still: most of us do not even see that we have a problem. We laugh at talk of demons, but fail to see them hovering over ourselves. To use the current jargon, we all want to be 'affirmed', not denied. But sometimes criticism and even condemnation of ourselves is the only way to the truth, the only way to healing. Even Christ had to go into the desert. Monasticism, whether in the form of the solitary hermit like Antony or in its later more communitarian pattern, at least alerts us to the need for such a radical challenge both to our own lives and to that of the wider society in which we are set.

Too often divine judgement is presented in exclusively negative terms. The image of the desert reminds us of how it can be so much more. If we heed its critique, it can lead us to an alternative city, one in which, like the blossoming desert in which Paul and Antony share a loaf, no one is left short, no one bereft – as the Gospel puts it, with twelve baskets more than we need (Mk 6.43).

5

Hilary and Athanasius

Wrestling to make doctrine relevant

Although contemporaries, Hilary and Athanasius are a contrasting pair. In the case of Athanasius we know quite a lot about his life, whereas with Hilary our knowledge is negligible. Almost certainly Hilary was canonized for what he wrote rather than for how he behaved. Nowadays his name is virtually forgotten except in some ancient institutions such as the Law Courts in London and Oxford University which designate the early months of the year as the Hilary Term (his feast day falls on January 13th). A convert to Christianity, he was married with a daughter when he was made Bishop of Poitiers by popular acclaim in 353. Most of the intervening period before his death fourteen years later was taken up with defending the full divinity of Christ. Though they never met, it is at this point that his life intersects with the eastern Athanasius, working in Egyptian Alexandria, then the second largest city in the Roman Empire (after Rome itself). Together, they made the decisive contribution to what came to be understood as Christian orthodoxy on the question of how Christ's humanity and divinity were to be understood.

The Emperor Constantine was the first Roman emperor to be converted to Christianity. It was to resolve disputes within the Church as to how Christ's divinity should be understood that he summoned in 325 what was to be the first universal council of the Church, meeting at Nicaea, near his new capital.

The council produced the first version of what we now call the Nicene Creed, said in most churches at every Sunday celebration of the eucharist. This asserts the complete equality of the Father and Son in the phrase 'True God of true God, begotten not made, of one being [or substance] with the Father.'

That last phrase was much agonized over, as it introduced into the definition of Christianity for the first time a non-biblical phrase, the Greek word *homoousios*. More conservative Christians objected, not only because the phrase was unscriptural, but also because it seemed to go against the obvious meaning of some key texts, such as John 14.28 ('The Father is greater than I') or I Corinthians 15.28 ('When all things are subjected to him, then the Son himself will also be subjected to him who put all things under him'). This led to a preference among many for the term *homoiousios*, meaning 'of like or similar substance', rather than the bald *homoousios*, 'of the same substance'.

Gibbon in his *Decline and Fall of the Roman Empire* ridicules such a dispute over a single letter, the Greek 'i' or iota. Certainly today many would endorse that criticism, and by no means all would be non-believers. Is it not disputes like this which have led to the term 'theological' being used in popular culture of all that is most abstruse and difficult to comprehend? Indeed, at the time the great majority of Christians seemed to have wished to adopt a less precise and less technical formula, and in this they were followed by the new emperor himself, Constantius II. He was the son of Constantine and sole emperor from 350, following the death of his two brothers, with whom the government of the empire had originally been shared.

The fact that the Nicene formula survived is largely the work of these two individuals, in the eastern empire Athanasius, and Hilary in the west. Athanasius had to endure exile from his diocese no less than five times. The loneliness of his struggle is epitomized in the common description of him as '*Athanasius contra mundum*' – Athanasius against all the world. Hilary too was exiled, though only once. At a provincial meeting at

Béziers in 356, along with only one other bishop, he refused to join in the general condemnation of Athanasius, and so was exiled to Phrygia, in central Turkey, where he spent the time learning Greek, discussing theology with the Greeks there who knew some, and also writing his measured response to those with whom he disagreed.

Nowadays we would need to acknowledge that neither he nor Athanasius had any real understanding of the way in which appreciation of the full significance of Christ is still developing within the Scriptures (with John's Gospel as the most developed). Indeed, in some passages the stronger case really does seem to lie with their opponents (e.g. Mk 6.5; Matt. 24.36; Jn 14.28). Of the two Athanasius had very much more the original, creative mind. But Hilary surpasses Athanasius in at least one respect: in his recognition that it is not the terms as such that make the difference – at one time he even proposed abandoning Nicaea – but what lies behind them. One of his earliest writings, his commentary on Matthew, may be used to illustrate the point.

For Hilary the significance of the story of the magi lies not so much in the factual events as in what they symbolize. They are a 'sacrament', a mysterious disclosure of the heart of what the incarnation was really all about. Wise men following the brightness of a star tells us of a new wisdom, a new knowledge of God that is now in our midst, one that demands the abandonment of our old ways, just as the magi were ordered to depart 'another way' rather than return to Herod's court. And that new knowledge, the symbolic mystery, is focused in the three gifts which they offer. Myrrh was used as part of the process of embalming the dead – to alleviate nasty smells – and so reminds us of the death to which the child (and all humanity) is called. Gold speaks of kings, and so of the judgement that same child one day will exercise. But it is the frankincense which provides the link, the real clue to what unites all three symbols. For incense speaks of the child as an object of worship, as divine, and it is only when we grasp this that the other two can then be linked together in a single sacramental unity. While it is as human that the child goes to his death, it is as divine that he rises once more to new life in the resurrection, and so can exercise judgement on all human beings whom he calls to share in that resurrection, in that new life.[10]

Not that Athanasius ignored such points, but he has a tendency to express himself in more technical, less engaged language. Perhaps the best-known phrase from his writings declares that 'God became human in order that human beings might become divine'. What he means is that there is nothing in us that is naturally immortal. As human beings we are all destined to death and the decay of sin. But God by becoming one of us has made a new reality possible: the defeat of sin, and life beyond the grave.

As Hilary might have put it, it is something which can be a reality for each and every one of us if only we are willing to identify with the sacramental, the symbolic reality that was Jesus' life, death and resurrection. That is again why for Hilary it is not the fact of Jesus' baptism that matters so much as that to which it points. When the heavens opened and declared a human being the Father's 'beloved Son', they opened the gate of heaven to us all. They declared us all God's children adopted by him through our baptism into Christ: as Hilary puts it, Christ's baptism is 'an image of the mystery prepared for *us*'.

And for that to be so it was important that no lesser reality was present than God himself: a reality *homoousios* – 'of the same substance' – with the Father. The sacrament, the symbol, the mystery of that human life was as the life of God himself in our midst, and it is that fact which can give us confidence to partake in the sacraments of today. The God who mediated a perfect human life in Christ continues to be with us, still offering that life for our enrichment and transformation.

Like all of us, Hilary and Athanasius of course made mistakes. Athanasius, for instance, nowhere acknowledges that Christ had a human soul; Hilary talks of Christ having a celestial body that knows the force of the passion, but not its pain. Clearly, neither had as yet drawn the full consequences of the incarnation. Even so, they went further than most of their contemporaries, insisting that the incarnation was not a half-way house; it was God himself fully entering into our condition. For standing so firm against their fellow Christians and thus creating the Church of today, we continue to remain in their debt.

6

John Chrysostom

A firebrand for the city's poor

'Has hell fire no end? I know that a chill comes over you even as I speak.' More often than not when one reads something from the past, what first strikes the attention is the difference between then and now. Readers are unlikely ever to have encountered in a sermon they have heard words like those I have just quoted. Similarly, the more the nature of first-century Palestine is known, the more one becomes conscious of the great difference that exists from our own day. It was a world of peasant farmers, part of a poor and fairly minor province of the Roman Empire, with even its erstwhile capital now a cultural backwater compared to the many, very much larger cities which existed. But in due course Christianity did invade those major cities. By the fourth century, though the majority of the population was still pagan, it was the Empire's official religion, and clergy of cities at least ten times the population of the Jerusalem of Jesus' time were now being required to work in close intimacy with the imperial authorities. And sermons like the one from which I have just quoted were being preached. Yet, as we shall see, not all was different.

Two such large cities were Antioch, the main centre of trade routes between west and east, and Constantinople, the new imperial capital. The most famous preacher of the ancient world – nicknamed 'the Golden Mouthed', John 'Chrysostom' – was, successively, one of the leading priests of Antioch for twelve years (386–98) and then, reluctantly, bishop of the capital city for a further six (398–404). A huge body of sermons which he delivered to those two cities survives, including one on the first letter of John from which the reference to hell with which I began is taken. Yet hell is in fact seldom mentioned in John's writings as a whole. Clearly, here he is using an all too obvious strategy to prompt his readers towards greater self-reflection. More commonly his tactics are rather more subtle.

But shock he most certainly did. For someone like me who likes his food and drink I know of no better way of getting myself to squirm in embarrassment than to read a few pages of one of John's polemical descriptions of the glutton at work. He is much better than any diet plan! However, he had in his sights something much larger than merely personal self-indulgence. He saw both cities dominated by the gospel of grab, and it is the lust for money, the lust for possessions, and the terrible impact such lust has on the poor, which he makes the repeated focal point of his critique.

The fact that Chrysostom's day falls only two days after the Feast of the Conversion of St Paul (January 25th) could scarcely be more appropriate, since for him Paul is the great Christian hero, the greatest saint who ever lived according to one of the panegyrics he wrote in praise of Paul. John had spent two years in the desert and he knew every word of Paul off by heart. But the Paul he thereby discovered was not the Paul of the Reformation – 'justification by faith', 'faith before works' and so forth – nor the Paul of the modern biblical scholar. It was the Paul of radical personal and social action. For John the heart of Paul's message is that the root of all sin is self-centredness; pride is the worst of faults because it cuts us off from a sense of dependency on others and thus also upon God. Therefore the only real test of the Christian is in action, in reaching out beyond ourselves, in love and in generosity. So a faith that shows no concern for the poor is in John's eyes no faith at all.

The problem, in his view, is not the faith we already have, but rather our failure to see its practical applications: that it summons us out of ourselves. As he expresses it at one point, 'possessions' in Greek (*chremata*) literally means 'what we need or use', whereas when things go wrong, what happens is that they use us; we are turned in on ourselves. As the sermon on hell observes, such covetousness makes us lower than the beasts: 'For beasts and wolves, when they are satiated, leave off their kind of eating: but these know not any satiety. And yet for this cause God made us hands, to assist others, not to plot against them'.

I began by emphasizing the difference between the ancient world and our own, but the more we heed Chrysostom's detailed descriptions of such corruption, the more after all we hear ourselves and our own society. For instance, he tells us of the fashion for silk lacing for one's shoes as a way of showing one's wealth. But how does that differ from our own designer labels, whether on shoes or elsewhere? Again, he tells of beggars on the streets whom the wealthy pass by. Has anything changed? He observes the passion for the racecourse and betting, and how even the churches empty on Good Friday in order to get to the Hippodrome in time. Enthusiasm for the National Lottery may be waning, but the parallels remain. Again, he talks of exorbitant profits made by those in positions of power, both those in government and in business. In a nation where the gap between the highest and lowest paid is widening, and has already surpassed that of Germany and Japan, can we really claim any superiority?

What fools we are – no different from the citizens of Antioch and Constantinople all those centuries ago. In the end Chrysostom's critique overstepped itself. He attacked the Empress Eudoxia twice, once for 'like Jezebel' manipulating the law in order to acquire new property and once for having a statue of herself placed outside the very door of the capital's cathedral. That was enough to secure his downfall, particularly when combined with the unscrupulous machinations of Theophilus, the bishop of Alexandria, the second largest city of the empire and centre of the corn trade. Chrysostom was exiled to the Black Sea and, though Eudoxia was soon dead, her weak husband Arcadius pursued the vendetta. Initially the hope was that Chrysostom would be killed by the bands of Isaurian bandits in the area, but when that failed a forced winter march in the snow finally did the trick, in 407.

Chrysostom thus died for his vision of Pauline theology. That is unlikely to be our fate, but it is only fair to Chrysostom that I end with that note of judgement with which his sermon (and this reflection) began. He had no doubt whatsoever about the gentleness and compassion of God and thus of the gentleness and compassion required of us, especially to those who do us wrong. Expert on Scripture that he was, he observed that the literal reading of the four gospels which he favoured (this being the fashion at Antioch) requires two cleansings of the temple, one at the beginning of Jesus' ministry (John) and one at the end (Mark). Taking that fact as his starting point, he observes that it is only in the second and later one that Jesus, with his patience now exhausted, uses particularly harsh language – 'den of thieves' rather than 'market' (Mk 11.17; contrast Jn 2.16). Even then he curses only a fig tree (Mk 11.12–14, 20–2) and not any human being, in Chrysostom's view as a warning of what God is entitled to do to human beings but longs not to.

Hell is thus for him a theology of last resort. The introduction of two Temple cleansings may be wildly improbable, but at least he uses it to speak of divine compassion, of the longing of God to bring in the lost. Even those who have abused their privileges may still get to heaven through the generous pleadings of the poor. Thus, although threats of hell may seem to speak of a vanished world, the continuities and relevance are still there: we all stand under a gentle judge, but a judge nonetheless, and one who is the friend of the poor.

7

Columba

Celtic dislocation

Many readers will, I'm sure, be familiar with Bede's story of why Pope Gregory decided to send a mission to England. Seeing some handsome slaves for sale in the Roman market, he asked who they were and being told that they were Angles (English), he replied 'not Angles but *angeli*' (angels). So in due course when he became pope, the mission to England was launched under Augustine, Canterbury's first bishop, with Augustine setting foot on English soil in 597. That same year, a few weeks later but several hundred miles further north, a faithful white horse, used for carrying milk, detected its master's declining years. Drawing close to him, it put its head in his bosom, as its own animal way of lamenting its master's impending death. That master was St Columba, founder and abbot of Iona. It is really to Iona in the Western Isles and not to Canterbury that northern England owes the greater debt, since it was Aidan – sent from Iona – who was the first to achieve missionary success in the north-east.

Augustine in fact represented the newer, more centralized Roman order, whereas Columba and Aidan sprang from the Celtic Christianity that was to yield to that order at the Synod of Whitby in 664. So 9 June 597 marks more than just the death of Columba: with the arrival of Augustine, the year also heralds the dawn of a new dispensation, the Roman centralized approach. Some of the disagreements that divided Roman and

Celt may now only occasion in us a wry smile, such as their arguments about the best way of calculating Easter or rival views on a monk's proper tonsure – how he should have his hair cut (close-shaven round the edge or on top). Even what initially seem more substantial issues, such as the Celtic practice of subordinating bishops to the power of the monasteries, may possibly have had more to do with tribal structure (notions of *coarbship* or 'coinheritance' among the Celts) than with any deep questions of theology. Even so, there do certainly remain some areas where we can still learn from the Celts, and not just the cult of nature with which they are currently so commonly and not always very accurately identified. The life of Columba may be used to make the point.

Given that Columba is the Latin for 'dove' (his Gaelic name *Columcille* had meant 'dove of the Church'), his first appearance on history's stage is a surprisingly bloody one. In what must be one of the earliest recorded instances of a dispute over copyright, the story goes that the Battle of Cooldrevny took place because Columba, then a prince of Donegal, had made an unauthorized copy of a valuable manuscript. So great were the casualties that he was sent into exile. But if initially this was under duress, the Irish *Life* is quick to stress the exile's subsequent voluntary character. Indeed, a parallel is drawn with Abraham, also summoned by God to leave familiar pastures for a strange land (Gen. 12.1). It was what the ancient Irish called a 'white martyrdom', a separation from home and kin to serve God in unfamiliar surroundings, and indeed it is on this version that the Latin *Life* by St Adamnán places exclusive stress.

Initially, it may not seem very promising material for our own day. So much of the emphasis appears negative, with stress on self-denial and so forth. But there is rather more than first meets the eye. To us martyrdom immediately suggests suffering and death, but, as we noted in an earlier chapter, its root meaning is 'witness,' and so what such white martyrdom was really about was witnessing to an alternative perception of the world. Its real heart lay in what we might call the dislocation of the sensibilities that were involved, the deliberate shock to the system as it were, such that new patterns of perception could then emerge. The imposed unfamiliar surroundings led one to a new appreciation of the value, context and purpose of one's life. Most readers will have experienced at some point in their own lives the involuntary jolt that has had exactly this effect; for example, through the death of a loved one, or some unexpected act of kindness from a stranger. But what the concept of white martyrdom enjoins upon us is that we should positively invite such jolts. But how, and what might be the benefits?

Consider first the Celtic idea of having an *ammchara* or 'soul-friend'. This was the precursor of the clerical confessor, but then (as now) anyone, lay or clerical, can fulfil the task. The point is the absolute need of each and every one of us to share our deepest selves with another person, so that we can hear how we ourselves are seen. All too easily we get into ruts, into supposing that there is no way now in which we can change, no way in which we need to be challenged. Just recall how depressing it can often be to listen to another's description of themselves, when we know full well how totally askew from reality it in fact all is. But might that not also be true of each and every one of us? So do we not all need soul-friends to give us that jolt, to dislocate our sensibilities, so that we can relocate and thus continue to increase our self-understanding and so grow both as human beings and as children of God?

Yet why, like Columba, leave one's native patch to achieve such growth? My experience may also be the reader's, but certainly several times in my life I have been disconcerted by strangers asking me basic questions about the place in which I happened to live, and not knowing the answer. There is a sense in which the local – unlike the tourist – simply takes certain things for granted, and so it is often the foreigner, the wanderer, who better appreciates the local beauty spots. Pagan Celtic religion already had a deep sense of the divine in nature. But there is no doubt that the peregrinations of the Celtic saints produced an intensification of that sense. Initially Adamnán's *Life of Columba* is very disconcerting because it seems to contain nothing else save instances of second sight, miracle and vision, as though all that interested the author were demonstrations of Columba's power. However, to dismiss it as legendary – as indeed much of it may well be – is equally to miss the point. For what matters is not the power or lack of it, but what the images are primarily intended to convey, that is the sense of intimacy discovered by such dislocation: God in every thought, God in every bush, God in every stone. Whether it is restraining the Loch Ness monster – Columba provides our first allusion – healing a crane damaged in flight or reassuring an aged retainer horse, the whole world for Columba had become alive with God.

And that can become our experience as well. We too can cease to be frightened by silence, switch off the television and listen for the still, small voice of God. We too can take a walk in the countryside and hear the trees whispering of the Creator who made them or listen to the gentle, regular lap of the waves telling of the calm and peace which only God can bring – to put it in words which could conceivably be Columba's own, 'the heaving waves of the glittering ocean as they chant their melody to their Father'. However achieved, one thing is clear. Clinging too closely to the familiar is a mistake. Dislocation may hurt, but it can also be profoundly enriching and draw us into a greater intimacy with God.

8

Aidan and Augustine

Destructive pride

I recall once reading a letter from an Anglican bishop in which he remarked (perhaps with tongue in cheek) that Michael Ramsey could not possibly be described as a saint. After all, he had not been very good at keeping appointments, and letters he was not keen to answer had the nasty habit of disappearing down the side of his armchair, and so getting forgotten. If the bishop in question really was being serious, it does demonstrate how naïve some of us are on the question of sanctity. Some 'saints' have of course been wrongly canonized, sometimes for political reasons. But even if we exclude these, it would still be the case that in the vast majority similar faults to those of Michael Ramsey were also to be found. For sanctity is not about perfection, but about the striving for perfection, about living so intimately with God − even given one's faults − that one communicates to others something of the presence of the divine, of the love that can also fire our own souls. Sometimes such a person does so precisely because his faults are so obvious, his inadequacies so like our own; while with others it is the very contrast that brings home to us the vision of God. To illustrate what I mean, let me take two such saints, both from the sixth century but very different in many other ways.

The first is St Augustine of Canterbury, who embarked on his mission to England in 596, finally landing in England in 597. The Collect for his day speaks of him 'taking the good news of your Son to the dark places of the world'! It had been a long journey with uncertain prospects, so perhaps it is not altogether surprising that this is exactly how Augustine and his companions felt at the prospect of England. Indeed, the historian Bede tells us that they had only gone 'a short distance on their journey' when 'they became afraid, and began to consider returning home, for they were appalled at the idea of going to a barbarous, fierce and pagan nation, of whose very language they were ignorant'.[11] However, Pope Gregory urged them on, and in due course the local king Ethelbert is converted and Augustine duly established at Canterbury.

Yet even with all that achieved Augustine still emerges as a rather timid man. Thus, despite the enormous pressures that there must have been on the Pope's time, Augustine still insists on referring back to Rome numerous questions of detail: for example, 'May a man marry his stepmother?', 'Should an expectant mother be baptized?', 'Is it necessary for other bishops to be present at a consecration?', 'What penalty should attach to the robbing of churches?' Bede has preserved for us Pope Gregory's answers, which are by no means one-line replies. In fact one cannot help but be impressed by their pastoral sensitivity. In the nicest possible way, Augustine is reprimanded for being a prig – for being far too much of a legalist in morals, and not looking enough to the underlying motives and practical situations of the individuals concerned.

There then are two major character faults that Augustine had: he was timid and priggish. Yet despite that he was able to do great things for God, to win over the Anglo-Saxons to Christianity. So we ought to learn at least this much from his life, that if only we trust in God then he can do great things with us, however inadequate others may think us or we may feel ourselves to be. It is not at all a matter of our having to become perfect before God can do anything with us or through us. Rather, if only we will let him, God's grace can achieve much in and through us despite all our faults.

But even with all that said, mention of Augustine's faults is still not at an end. There is one more to which I wish to draw the reader's attention. I do this not to revel in exposing so great – and so saintly – a man, but because this particular fault of Augustine's is one from which again we all suffer: one which can often produce terrible consequences within a Christian community, as indeed it did in the case of Augustine. This is the refusal to yield an inch to one's opponent when one knows oneself to be in the right, even though this would appear to be the only way of effecting a reconciliation.

Augustine's significance for history lies in his missionary work in the south of England, in winning over the Anglo-Saxon or English-speaking peoples of that part of the country. However, as we saw in the last chapter, the Celts further north pursued a range of practices which no longer prevailed in the rest of Europe, and Augustine therefore saw it as part of his duty to win them over to conformity with Rome. A united Church could not possibly have two different ways of calculating Easter; nor did it make sense for monasteries to have more power than bishops, since this could so easily lead to competition between the different religious houses, which would be prevented if they were all under a single authority. So there is no doubt in my mind that Augustine was entirely right in this dispute. Nonetheless he went entirely the wrong way about resolving it.

A conference was arranged between the two parties. What, however, Augustine did not know was that the Celts were already thinking of giving in, and had consulted one of their hermits about the rightness of doing so. He proposed a very simple test to determine whether Augustine was a man of God or not. His suggestion was: 'Arrange that Augustine and his followers arrive first at the place appointed for the conference. If he arises courteously as you approach, rest assured that he is a servant of Christ and so do as he asks. But if he ignores you and does not rise, then, since you are in the majority, do not comply with his demands'. Inevitably what happens is that Augustine does not rise from his chair, and so the dispute lingers on for another sixty years, until the Synod of Whitby in 664. All because Augustine would not meet the Celts half-way. He remained seated because he wanted them to concede not only the superiority of his arguments but also the superiority of his person. He wanted, as it were, to rub it in that he had won.

Now contrast this with the behaviour half a century earlier of one of the best-known Celtic missionaries from Iona, St Aidan. An earlier attempt to win Northumbria had failed, and it is Aidan who correctly identified the reason. At a conference convened to discuss the causes of the failure, he himself declares: 'Brothers, it seems to me that you were too severe on your ignorant hearers. You should have followed the practice of the apostles . . . and gradually nourished them with the word of God until they were . . . able to follow the loftier precepts of Christ'. In other words, Aidan clearly saw the need to meet people half-way even when one is in the right. And of course that is exactly what our Lord himself did. He came to earth not in glory, lording it over us all, but as one of us. Can we therefore do anything else?

It is also of Aidan that Bede tells the beautiful story of his giving away to a beggar the horse King Oswyn had bestowed on him to help him with his missionary journeys. It is clear that Bede had unbounded admiration for his compassion, gentleness and humility. The only negative feature he mentions is Aidan's failure to follow the Roman rule for the observance of Easter, and here he does hint at a possible fault; for he traces this to Aidan being too much under 'the influence of his own tribe', as he puts it. Had too much conformity or local pride prevented him from seeing the wider arguments?

A small fault perhaps compared to the timidity, priggishness and concern for status we find in Augustine. But both alike were saints afire with God's spirit, and both can teach us in our own lives. From Augustine we can learn that God can work with the most ordinary of us: there is none beyond his trans-forming power; while even those few of us who reach Aidan's heights need to learn that no one is above correction, that if only we will listen there may be a still wider and more glorious vision awaiting us. Recognition of a journey that never ends on this side of the grave: there is sanctity, and there too our goal.

9

Gregory the Great

The papacy that might have been

Bede leaves us in no doubt about his great admiration for Gregory the Great, the pope responsible, as we have seen, for sending Augustine as a missionary to England. Bede too emphasizes the importance of his major writings, which were indeed to be definitive for the future shape of medieval theology. He also makes much of his saintly character, in particular his concern for the poor. Yet for all his praise Bede fails to note what seems to me Gregory's greatest claim to fame, that which really entitles Christians to continue to call him 'the Great'. It is on the reasons for his entitlement to this description that I want to focus here. In the process the extent of the contrast between secular and religious estimates of greatness should emerge with some force.

'The lofty tree under whose shade the nations of the earth had reposed, was deprived of its leaves and branches, and the sapless trunk was left to wither on the ground.'[12] So runs a famous sentence of Gibbon, describing the sad state of the city of Rome in which Gregory grew up. A city that had once boasted a population of a million inhabitants was now reduced to a mere 30,000; the capital had long since vanished to the east, to Constantinople; even the little of Italy that was still in imperial hands was governed from Ravenna, and not Rome; Lombard raids were constantly to be feared, and brigands terrorized the countryside, making food supplies uncertain. In

53

Gregory's own words: 'we see groaning everywhere: cities are destroyed, fortifications overthrown, the fields bare of men . . . [and] almost no one remains in the city or countryside'.[13]

While still a layman Gregory rose to be the principal imperial official within the city, carrying the title of 'prefect'. Yet he gave it all up to become a monk, giving away his personal wealth in the process, in order to found seven monasteries. But he was soon pulled out of seclusion in order to be the new pope's ambassador to the imperial court at Constantinople. This function he performed for seven years, not long before himself being elected pope in 590. He was only to hold office for fourteen years, but in that short space of time he set the pattern for the future development of the papacy, a pattern with which we are still living today. Not only did he by default take over many imperial functions within the city, but through emissaries and correspondence he sought to shape the behaviour of the entire Christian world.

Almost all of this he achieved by moral authority rather than by temporal power. It is, after all, rather hard to resist the upbraidings of someone who applies even stricter standards to himself! Not surprisingly perhaps, one example of this stems from his position as the first monk to be pope. He regularly intervened to restrain local bishops from exercising too much control over the monasteries in their area; the result was that, although worldwide religious orders were not yet on the horizon, already with Gregory we have the beginnings of the growth of a primary monastic allegiance to the papacy, over against the local diocesan bishop or national leader.

In short, it is from Gregory's period as pope that we should date both the rise of a papacy with strong centralizing tendencies and one which treats as its own personal fief the area around Rome. His namesake Gregory VII – Hildebrand – making an emperor do penance in the snow is still four centuries off, and more than 1000 years in the future is the nineteenth-century doctrine of papal infallibility; but certainly in the first thousand years of Christianity it was Gregory more than anyone else who contributed to that authoritarian and centralizing tendency.

Living after an event, it is so easy to think of what ensued from it as inevitable. But in sixth-century Italy this was really far from obvious. Power had moved east, and Rome was, as we have seen, really a provincial backwater. In fact, we find Gregory trying in vain to persuade some of Rome's leading citizens not to flee to Ravenna or even to distant Constantinople, where Latin was at this time still the official language. It is also at this time that the Patriarch of Constantinople first abrogates to himself the description 'ecumenical' or 'universal', a designation maintained to this day. To most in the empire that title probably now seemed entirely appropriate. So it is not hard to envisage a very different scenario having developed from the one we know today, with instead the much looser relation which characterizes the various autonomous churches that make up eastern Christendom applying here also in the west, and the Bishop of Rome much more like a first among equals, or perhaps even subordinate to the eastern patriarch.

But western Christendom in the end followed a quite different pattern, not least because the papacy moved to fill the vacuum created by the retreat of the empire eastwards. Yet the irony is that, despite the many ways in which Gregory contributed to such a development, he did so by default, for he had no such conception in mind. Indeed, so depressed was he by conditions in Italy that he was absolutely convinced that the end of the world was at hand. His motivation in transforming the papacy had thus nothing at all to do with setting it on its future centralizing course; it was rather all a matter of ensuring that he had done a task well: ensuring, so far as possible, that the Church that eagerly awaited the return of its Saviour was presented to that Saviour as being as blameless as possible. And it is this motivation which can help explain the focus of each of his three major works. His *Dialogues* are concerned to overawe us with a sense of the presence of God through vision and miracle. One key example he takes is the life of someone from his own century: St Benedict, the founder of the west's most important religious order. His *Moralia* faces the issue of suffering by reinterpreting the Book of Job. Job becomes a Christ figure who can help to make troubled times more intelligible and manageable. Finally, his *Pastoral Guide* tries to ensure that church leaders will set an appropriate example in the face of the expectation of Christ's coming soon in judgement.

Such 'greatness' by accident may well be all too much for some readers. After all, it will be said, his own motivation was based on a false belief that the world was soon to end. Again, while he may have set in train the process that led to the sort of papacy that eventually developed, without a weak empire that would never have happened, and so it is wrong to give Gregory much of the credit. Christians, though, should be wary of basing a critique on such ways of evaluating greatness. Gregory's aim was humbly to serve God, and more distant consequences (which in any case he could scarcely have fore-seen) were not his concern. Nor was he by any means unusual in believing in the imminence of the world's end. It is a con-viction that is not uncommon in the New Testament itself (e.g. Mk 13.14–27; 1 Cor. 7.29). No, Gregory is great not because he got everything right, but because of the way he con-scientiously sought to do what was needful at the time, and in a way that showed love and compassion for those for whom he was responsible. The secular focus is on his role in the growth of papal power, however unintentional; the religious focus on a life of faithful service that trusted God into the unknown. Not for nothing is he the first pope to describe himself as *servus servorum Dei* – 'servant of the servants of God'.

Even today church leaders could read with profit his *Pastoral Guide*, with its shrewd mixture of discernment and humility. A constantly reiterated theme is the need for both self-discernment and the adaptation of all that one does to the condition of those with whom one is dealing. Surviving to this day is the table upon which he shared his meals with the poor in the Lateran Palace, which Constantine had built for the popes. Direction and humility thus went hand in hand. In fact, all these interventions in the wider Church were motivated by tireless search for service, and not by lust for power. In his view, among his fellow-bishops he was merely a first among equals, and what he sought was not greater control over them but that they should act as Christ would have wished them to act.

The net result was that he was tolerant of a degree of diversity that would have been quite unacceptable to most of his successors. A good example of this is the way in which, despite his abhorrence of pagan classical literature, he willingly adopted a gradualist approach to contemporary paganism. Indeed, in one of his sermons he finds endorsement for this in Scripture. He argues that the reason why the wise men were given a star whereas angels appeared to the shepherds was because the wise men, being pagans, could only be approached indirectly through signs.[14] It was the same approach that he applied in England. Mellitus, Augustine's companion and successor, was urged to adapt pagan shrines and even to allow the continuance of animal sacrifice.[15]

Thus, this Gregory was of quite a different stamp from the highly authoritarian papacy that was eventually to emerge – ironically in part because of his own actions – in the Middle Ages. His objective remained a life of ministry to others, and if he got some things wrong, this if anything only intensified the sense of urgency in his actions. In this world Christians must walk by faith and not by sight. Much of God's plans for the world's future will necessarily remain hidden from us. Sadly, all too often modern church leaders long for a control that simply cannot be had. Gregory saw something more important: encouraging others in the growth of a self-confident faith that does not constantly rely on instruction from others. Service that makes one's own self ultimately redundant – that is true service, a real *servus servorum Dei*.

Part II: The Medieval Church

10

Margaret of Scotland

Hidden debts to others

Probably born in Hungary, Margaret was an English princess, part of the ancient royal stock that had been permanently displanted when William the Conquerer seized the throne of England in 1066. She became the second wife of Malcolm III of Scotland, nicknamed Canmore or 'Big-head'. Rough and illiterate, he constituted quite a contrast to his devout and gentle queen. Even so, readers may be tempted to cast Margaret equally into a past and best forgotten age, when I reveal that her most treasured possession was a supposed splinter from the cross on which Jesus had suffered and died. This was encased in a jewelled cross known as the black rood, and subsequently held before the face of each Scottish king as he died until it was captured from David II at the Battle of Neville's Cross in 1346. Neville's Cross is now a suburb of the city of Durham. So into that cathedral went the rood along with an alleged tooth of Margaret, and then kept there and venerated until the Reformation.

Medieval superstition at its worst, you may say. Why single out something so trivial as a tooth, or fly in the face of all historical probability and venerate something as implausible as a 'true relic' of Christ's cross? Many will turn with relief to the only memento that has survived into our day, her copy of the Gospels, rediscovered in 1887 and now in the possession of the Bodleian Library at Oxford. It would be a natural temptation to contrast our own sophistication in valuing something so beautiful and well authenticated with the naïve incredulity of the Middle Ages. But if that is our tendency, we congratulate ourselves, I believe, too quickly. For there is something important to learn from even those apparently trivial relics of tooth and splinter. To sketch what this might be, I want to invite the reader to consider two very different estimates of the significance of Margaret's life.

The traditional view is that her achievement was considerable: by the time she died in 1093 she had both civilized the Scots and at last brought them fully within the orbit of the Catholic church. Steeped first in the piety of the court of St Stephen of Hungary and then of St Edward the Confessor, fleeing north from William the Conqueror she brought to the court of Malcolm III a wisdom and a religious sensibility which he lacked. Summoning Benedictine monks from Canterbury she established a splendid new monastery at Dunfermline, upon which the Durham stonemasons were first to test their new skills north of the border. Iona was refounded, and St Andrews was made a major pilgrimage centre, with a ferry provided free of charge to carry the travellers over the River Forth, and overnight shelters nearby in the village that to this day bears her name; Queensferry. Then under her guidance councils were called to root out the kind of idiosyncratic Celtic practices that had been successfully banned in the north of England four centuries previously at the Synod of Whitby in 664. Monastic reform and firm episcopal government thus became the order of the day, and Scotland at last came into line with the wider Church on numerous points of detail. For instance, Lent now began on Ash Wednesday instead of the following Monday (Sundays having hitherto been counted as part of the Lenten fast), and Scots ceased to shy away from taking communion on Easter Day because of alleged unworthiness.

Many modern historians, however, now want to tell a rather different tale.[16] There is much irony in this dispute, inasmuch as we should be better informed about Margaret than about almost any other figure of the eleventh century, since we have a contemporary biography, written by Turgot, a former prior of the Benedictine Abbey that was at this time attached to Durham Cathedral. Increasingly, however, his reliability is being doubted – not that Queen Margaret's saintliness is thereby destroyed, but rather the extent of her achievement is called into question. The list of reforms Turgot mentions is suspiciously like those which he himself tried to impose upon the Scots when he became Bishop of St Andrews a decade after Margaret's death, while he is curiously vague about the councils which the queen allegedly convened, failing to mention where they met, which bishops were there and so on. Again, Benedictine monks may have been invited to Dunfermline, but there is no evidence of Benedictine communities in Scotland until well after Margaret's death. Indeed, there is evidence to suggest that Margaret actually fostered the old Celtic way of monastic life, in her patronage of the hermits known as culdees.

So the prevailing view now is that Turgot deliberately exaggerated, in order to please the person who commissioned the biography, Margaret's daughter, Edith (or Maud as she became known when she married Henry I of England). In fact, it was Margaret's son, King David I, who was really responsible for the religious transformation of Scotland, a transformation still visible as one tours the Scottish Borders and observes the magnificent ruins of abbeys he founded, such as Jedburgh, Melrose and Kelso. In reality, her two children, the canonized David and 'good Queen Maud' as she was popularly known, almost certainly achieved far more than their mother, a mother in any case whom they would not have known beyond their early childhood years.

But are we right to leave matters there? Let me return for a moment to those trivial relics with which we began, the tooth and the splinter. Nowadays, we love to see ourselves as our own creation, formed and shaped entirely by our own choices. But is this not pure fantasy? Consider two instances from my own life. Picture a little boy, another David – that's me! – saying goodbye to an elderly lady called Winifred who is leaving her northern home. Politely I remark that I look forward to seeing her again one day when I visit London. Her response drew me up with a start: 'David, I shall be dead before then, but you *will* see me again'. Then that same David, now a student looking after a project in a deprived council estate. A knock at the door, and there is little Alexander, a boy of four or five, with a bunch of flowers stolen from neighbours' gardens. Handing them over he says: 'I want you as my dad'. Both incidents had a major impact upon the development of my life. It was the elderly Winifred who first tore down for me the curtain between heaven and earth; it was little Alex who made me realize that the absolute moral blacks and whites by which I had hitherto lived just did not work. Yet it is unlikely that either Winifred or Alex kept in their memory the respective incidents with which I associate them. Indeed, given Alex's dreadful family background it is all too probable that he is now a hardened criminal. Even so, my debt to him remains incalculable.

The point I am trying to convey is that for better or worse we are all dependent on one another. We only partly shape ourselves; the rest comes from others, in ways that our bene-factors often little appreciate themselves. That is an intuition which I would suggest the other David, the saint and the king, and his sister, Maud, fully realized. They brought about larger transformations in their own time, but it was their mother Margaret who was entitled to the ultimate credit for making them who they were.

And so finally to the tooth and splinter that once adorned Durham Cathedral. Of course, there were bad motives in desiring to possess such relics, but there were also good. They spoke of the acknowledgment that we are not just individuals, that an association with Margaret, however minimal, could make the people of Durham a better, a more Christian com-munity. Even as they stole the splinter from the defeated Scots, like little Alex they acknowledged a love and devotion that was greater than themselves both in Margaret herself and in that fragment of the cross which she and her son held as they died. And like Winifred their acts spoke of the curtain of heaven pulled back, as they sought Margaret's prayers and her influence upon their lives.

Instead, today all we do is admire a beautiful artefact in an Oxford library. The result is that the historical distance only serves to intensify our sense of the difference and contrasting individuality between Margaret and ourselves. What, then, has become of our belief in the body of Christ, with us seen as all only living in and through one another, because we all live in him? It is as families, as friends and as communities that we create one another. Give me the tooth and splinter any day.

11

Anselm of Canterbury

On entering other worlds

I recall once a fellow cleric reprimanding me for the way in which I had introduced a selection of Anselm's prayers. I had prefaced them by referring to Anselm as a Burgundian, whereas he observed – rightly – that Anselm had been born in Aosta, which is in Italy. In retrospect it seems to me that his way of putting things would have been less misleading than mine. But the remark did start me upon the present chain of reflections.

Italy of course did not exist as a distinct nation until the nineteenth century. In the eleventh century when Anselm was born, Aosta, though south of the Alps, was in fact part of the French kingdom and duchy of Burgundy (its status varied). Combined with the fact that his mother's family came from the Rhône, this helps to explain why Anselm saw his future north and not south of the Alps, and so why the first stage of his progression to Archbishop of Canterbury was as a pupil of Lanfranc at the monastery of Bec in Normandy. Understanding history thus involves efforts of imagination before we can comprehend worlds often quite different from our own.

The example I have given is of course a very minor one. In Anselm's case, however, the requirement extends much more widely. Let me therefore give two larger examples by way of preamble to the spiritual lesson that I wish eventually to draw from them. In the contemporary Church we are much pre-occupied by the issue of homosexuality. Anselm is someone whom several historians have enlisted in their cause, alleging that he himself was gay and sympathetic to those similarly inclined. Certainly, he owed his very appointment as Archbishop of Canterbury in 1093 to a promiscuous homosexual, William the Conqueror's son, William Rufus; but it is primarily in his letters that support for the contention is thought to exist. Here is the sort of thing Anselm writes to other men: 'My eyes long to see your face most beloved; my arms stretch out to your embraces, my lips long for your kisses ... Oh how my love burns in my marrow.'[17]

It all sounds absolutely conclusive until one recalls the medieval symbolism associated with the kiss, a symbolism in large part generated by the biblical book, the Song of Songs. A kiss was the crowning act in the profession of new monks and in the reconciling of penitents, while even in the secular context it was the normal conclusion to acts of homage or reconciliation between enemies. So what Anselm was really doing by these words was incorporating his correspondents in a total identity of purpose. In any case, his one meditation on human sexuality shows him to be worried by sexual desire as a diversion from real seriousness in religious commitment. That too helps explain why as archbishop he was such an enthusiast in trying to enforce the new ideal of universal clerical celibacy – uphill task though that was, with even at least one of his bishops (Roger of Salisbury) still married.

My second example concerns his attitude to the papacy. This was the period of the great investiture controversy, a dispute particularly associated with another Benedictine monk, Hildebrand, who ruled as Pope Gregory VII (1073–85), though the issue predated him and was not to reach a satisfactory resolution until the following century. What was at stake was the independence of the Church: whether in virtue of the lands that also went with bishoprics, secular rulers had the right to appoint senior clerics to their posts and in the process invest them with their symbols of authority – the ring and the staff – leaving only the confirmatory role to the consecration in church. Inevitably bound up with this in Hildebrand's mind was the desire for a more centralized Church and with it increased papal authority.

Rufus died in 1100, and was succeeded by his younger brother, Henry. Anselm had been present in Rome the previous year when Hildebrand's decrees against investiture had been renewed, and in 1100 he announced to the new king his refusal either to offer homage to Henry or to accept any bishops invested by him. It is actions such as this which have led many an historian to see in Anselm the future papalist, the sort of Catholic who forever defines himself by appeal to Rome. So in the nineteenth century the Anglican historian R. W. Church commented: 'Thus began that system ... of inviting foreign interference in our home concerns which grew to such a mischievous and scandalous height; and Anselm was the beginner of it'.[18]

But in the twentieth century another Anglican historian, Sir Richard Southern, summoned us to an even greater effort of imagination; to see Anselm in his own chosen context as at the ending of an age rather than at the beginning of a new one. The enforcing of the papal decrees had for him no more significant rationale than obedience to a higher authority, the same sort of conception that had also led him to ask permission of both the Duke of Normandy and the Archbishop of Rouen before accepting Canterbury. Indeed, astonishingly, until his visit to Rome in 1099 he seems to have been totally unaware of Hildebrand's earlier decrees, which dated back to 1078. Even then he still failed to equip himself with any of the normal entourage that would be the future pattern for senior clerics in the Church – lawyers and civil servants.

His vision lay quite elsewhere. Anselm was in love with a beautiful world; not our own, but another country beyond the stars. In marked contrast to our disordered world of sin and uncertainty stood its beauty and harmony, with God at its centre – a God who, in his famous definition, is that than which nothing greater, nothing more marvellous can be thought, a being in whose essence there is no dysfunction, no conflict, and whose every action in this world proceeds either from a sense of necessity or fittingness. That is to say, whenever that Being impinges upon our world, he brings with it order, beauty, and harmony in all he does. Determined to convey that vision, Anselm does not hesitate to modify substantially the practice of his predecessors. Gone in his writings is all the clutter of appeals to earlier theological authorities, and in its place comes in his *Proslogion* the simplest of all arguments for God's existence (the so-called ontological argument), while in his *Cur Deus Homo* an account of Christ's role in our salvation is given in which every minute detail is seen to have its proper, its harmonious place.

But if there you have in brief his significance as a theologian, in the process I have produced one major distortion. For I spoke in terms of 'another country beyond the stars', as though this perfect reality were remote from us. But for Anselm it is our near neighbour, and nowhere does this emerge with greater clarity than in his prayers. Most are lively dialogues with the saints, with Christ's Mother, Mary Magdalene, John the Evangelist, Benedict, and so forth, and it was particularly in his attitude to the saints that he endeared himself to the local English Church. Like his predecessor Lanfranc, he too was a foreigner who knew no English, but, unlike Lanfranc who saw his role exclusively in correcting local custom, Anselm actively supported local cults, (such as those of Alphege and Dunstan at Canterbury). Indeed, there seems little doubt that in administering the see of Canterbury he saw himself as securing these saints' continued earthly concerns. For him only a thin veil separates this world and the next, and so wherever the order, beauty or justice of that other world is secured in this, such things can carry us through the veil to the next. Even as archbishop his heart and mind were really elsewhere. So the man who is undoubtedly internationally the best-known individual ever to have held the see of Canterbury was also among its least effective. Sanctity does not save us from incompetence, and there is no doubt that the Church of Anselm's day needed a very different, more worldly sort of archbishop.

Yet that is scarcely the right note on which to end. For it remains true that it is only by holding up to ourselves worlds and individuals very different to those of our own experience that we will ever learn, ever see the limitations of where we are, and discover instead where we might be. Aosta will never again become part of a kingdom of Burgundy; but we could once again live in a world where the Alps cease to be a significant frontier, just as the Welsh church, which under Anselm was first subjugated to English control, took long to regain its independence but finally did so in 1920. Likewise, never again will we live in a world in which the monk is seen as the only complete way of being a Christian; but we could once again live in a world where once more the veil falls and that harmonious other world becomes part of our own. Then with Anselm we too might be enabled both to cry: 'My understanding cannot take it in, it is too bright, I cannot receive it . . . dazzled as I am by its glory, mastered by its fullness, crushed by its immensity, confounded by its extent'; yet at the same time also utter the prayer: 'Let my tongue speak of it, let my heart love it, let my mouth preach it, let my soul hunger for it, my flesh thirst for it, and my whole being desire it, until I enter into the joy of the Lord.'[19]

12

Bernard and Abelard

With heart and mind

Let me offer the reader two contrasting images from medieval France, both from the second decade of the twelfth century. First, conjure up before your mind the mental fervour of the University of Paris, with the great genius of the day, Abelard, gathering as many as 5000 students about his rostrum at the École Sainte Geneviève, and soon eclipsing older seats of learning such as Notre-Dame and Saint-Victor. Now forty, he is at the height of his career and idolized by many of his pupils, not least the beautiful eighteen-year-old Heloïse, with whom he is secretly having an affair. Then, secondly, think of a twenty-two-year-old, handsome and wealthy nobleman, Bernard by name, living in the beautiful wine province of Burgundy, now contemplating how he will spend the rest of his life.

Neither story continues as you might expect. Not only is Abelard's affair discovered and his career ruined, but he is twice put on trial for heresy. Meantime, not only does Bernard turn his back on his father's wealth, but also he dismisses contemptuously such wealth and ease as the Church of his day might have afforded him. Cluny, the world's largest and most prosperous monastery, was nearby. But instead he sought admission to the new stricter version of the Benedictine order that had recently been founded at the place of the 'reeds', the desolate Citeaux. Eventually the new order was to take its name from this place – Cistercian – although Bernard himself went on to become abbot of another monastery with which his name is more commonly associated, Clairvaux.

It was the younger man, Bernard of Clairvaux, who was responsible for initiating those heresy trials against Abelard. Together they are the two most important intellectual figures of twelfth-century Europe; yet seldom can it have been the case that two men understood each other less. What we have in their conflict is two quite different ways of understanding the Christian faith. It is upon that clash and its significance that I want to reflect here. Only Bernard was canonized. Yet Abelard's name ought also to be remembered with respect.

Abelard's great aim was to render the Christian faith easily intelligible and defensible, and in pursuit of that aim he makes use of rigorous intellectual argument. Bernard, however, will have none of this. In his view the human task is to receive what God offers as a gift, not to question how. Typical, for instance, is his response to Abelard's question: 'Why did God do by blood [that is, by the death of Christ] what he could have done by word alone?' Bernard replies: 'It is permitted to me to know that it was so, but why it was so I am not permitted to know'.[20] In fact, for Bernard curiosity is the most dangerous of vices, the first and most serious step on the ladder of pride which leads to human self-destruction. That is how Eve and Satan fell; they wanted to have the kind of knowledge which gave them charge of their own destiny.[21] It is precisely for this reason that he so disliked Abelard's account of human responsibility in which all the stress is on correct intention. To Bernard it seemed that Abelard was suggesting that such control was within our compass, since in his view only then could we be held culpable or otherwise for what happens in the world.

But for Bernard what mattered was not what we control, but what we receive. Do we remain part of the corruption that is the inevitable lot of the human race, or are we even now being transformed by God's grace? For the latter to be so, what we need is not curiosity but self-knowledge, the awareness of our own lacks and thus of our need for God. It is at this point that we can see the heart of the contrast between the two men; for, if knowledge was the key for Abelard, for Bernard it was love. God has so made us that we naturally love ourselves. But the more we reflect on what love requires, he argues, the more we will see our need for God, and thus in due course love God for himself and not just for the benefits he gives us.[22]

It is into just such a framework that we must fit Bernard's understanding of the incarnation. God's love for us was such that he wanted wholly to identify with us in our human condition: he wanted an experiential knowledge of both our joys and our sufferings, so that by his wholly identifying with us, we might then wholly identify with him. Words for 'experience' in fact repeatedly appear in Bernard's writings: what he most desires is not an intellectual understanding of God like Abelard's, but a lived experiential identification of wills. As he observes, 'What God knew by nature from all eternity, he has now taught us through this temporal experience of his'. Indeed, such was his love for us that 'God now got to know by experience what hitherto he had only known by nature.'[23]

It is precisely the desire to reciprocate this identification of God with us that explains the austerity of Bernard's asceticism, an austerity so severe that it left him permanently in need of somewhere to vomit after eating: he wanted to share totally Christ's sufferings. But it also explains the more positive side: Christ as our lover, so beautifully developed in his eighty-six sermons on the Song of Songs. Admittedly, even here the vividness of the imagery may sometimes be too rich for us, as in his vision of Mary offering to feed him, like her son, with milk from her breasts. But these more puzzling features should not make us lose sight of his central vision: of Christ our lover, whose 'spiritual kiss' can transform our relationship not only with himself but also with one another. In Latin love and friendship are related words: *amor* and *amicitia*. Christ's love is thus there to transform us into one another's friends; for, as our Lord promised, 'you are my friends' (Jn 15.14).

And it was by the strength of such friendships, the strength of such love – a love not afraid to use mothering language both of himself and of God – that he transformed the Cistercian order into one of the great forces for good in medieval Europe. Already by his death in 1153 there were roughly 300 houses, including several in England still familiar through their ruins, such as at Rievaulx and Fountains. There was even a partial reconciliation with Abelard.

Yet, sadly, he never really understood Abelard's merits. This is all the more regrettable because in many ways he embodied precisely the kind of Christian Abelard had in mind, when he insisted that we must take greater responsibility for ourselves and our destinies. For Bernard was one of the great 'brokers' of Europe, constantly engaged, now in securing a peace treaty here, now in reprimanding a king there, even launching the Second Crusade – so busy outside the monastery that at times he even doubted whether he was really a monk, as he himself confesses in one of his letters. But even with all that business he failed to detect the dawn of a new, more questioning age. A mood with which Abelard was very much in tune, it was to become the norm with theologians like St Thomas Aquinas in the following century. Bernard thought that the old answers would do just as well. He even attacked Abelard for abandoning the old account of Christ's atonement for us that treated it as ransom payment. Yet several decades earlier this account had already been attacked by no less a figure than Anselm of Canterbury.

God wants both our minds and our hearts, not one or the other. It is not clear that Bernard ever learnt that lesson. Abelard most certainly did. The sufferings brought on by exposure of his affair refined his character. Both he and Heloïse entered the monastic life. They kept in contact, and he learned to love in a new way. 'Spiritual kisses' now passed between them in letters that record one of the most famous romances of the Middle Ages.

Among the many things Abelard did for Heloïse was write a complete hymnal for her convent. This includes a hymn composed for Saturday evenings, which we still sing today: 'O what their joy and their glory must be'. It speaks of a world where all life is a sabbath of praise to God:

Truly Jerusalem name we that shore
'Vision of peace,' that brings joy evermore.[24]

Bernard's prose style often achieves the lyricism of poetry. But it is to a contemporary and namesake of his, Bernard of Cluny, that we turn for a comparable hymn. From an extraordinary piece of nearly 3000 lines, entitled 'On Contempt of the World', comes a familiar hymn in our present hymn books: 'Jerusalem the golden'. Bernard of Cluny was a Benedictine, the order from which Bernard's own order of the Cistercians was derived. Is it just an accident that both hymns alike sing with one voice of the joys of heaven beyond the grave? May we not now imagine Bernard and Abelard with heart and mind united in the Jerusalem for which they both longed? Certainly, Abelard's hymn speaks of the heart's 'desire' fulfilled. If Bernard's fails to refer to the intellect, it was not long before the Cistercians too were seeking to make their own distinctive contribution to the new university learning, as with Rewley Abbey at Oxford (ironically, now the site of the city's railway station). God grant that our hearts and minds too may sing one and the same tune – God's melody, and none other.

13

Thomas à Becket and Hildebrand

Power and its ambiguities

The most popular place of pilgrimage in England in the Middle Ages was a politician's shrine, St Thomas à Becket's at Canterbury. Murdered in his own cathedral on the 29 December 1170 at the implicit behest of his own king and one-time friend, Henry II, within three years he had been canonized, and the following year (1174) Henry himself did public penance at his tomb. The murder was the culmination of a long series of disputes between king and archbishop, initiated by Becket's refusal to allow those in clerical orders to be tried before the civil courts, no matter how heinous their offence.

As such Thomas' death needs to be set against the tussle between Church and State which had then been going on throughout Europe for the past century, and which had effectively been set in motion by the great reforming Pope of the eleventh century, Hildebrand or – to give him his papal title – Gregory VII. Here too it is possible to focus the struggle on a single memorable event – Canossa. In the preceding centuries monarchs and local nobility had increasingly been appropriating the power to appoint clergy and bishops. Hildebrand realized that given such a situation the only realistic way of reforming the Church was if such power could be wrested from them. The emperor of the time (Henry IV) protested, and at a specially convened council declared the Pope deposed. Gregory in turn declared Henry excommunicated. Such were the resulting political pressures upon the Emperor that in the end he was forced to plead absolution from the Pope – as the story goes, waiting barefoot for three days in the snow before the castle of Canossa in northern Italy.

That was 28 January 1077. Yet go back 600 years earlier and we come to the exchange between State and Church which was taken as a model for all such subsequent clashes. The year is 390. At the head of the Roman Empire is Theodosius the Great, so-called as the restorer of the empire's fortunes after its crushing defeat by the Goths at the Battle of Adrianople in 378. His policy included settling some of these barbarians within the Empire, and in some instances even giving them positions of power and influence. One such, Botheric, as military commandant of Thessalonica in Greece made an unpopular decision which led to him being lynched by a local mob. So incensed was the emperor that he took a savage revenge, ordering the massacre of some 7000 citizens in the local arena. He met his match, however, in one bishop of the day, St Ambrose. A former civil governor, he was now Bishop of Milan, a city which at the time was effectively administrative capital of the western empire rather than Rome (it was nearer the frontiers which so desperately required guarding). Ambrose wrote to the emperor, refusing him communion till he repented of his decision. This Theodosius duly did. At Ambrose's insistence he was forced to issue a decree that in future no sentences of death should ever come into effect without thirty days' prior notice.

In each of the incidents I have just recounted it is possible to tell the story in radically different ways. I tried to offer a relatively neutral description. Without much further elaboration, however, it would be possible to present the events as great triumphs of faith over selfishness, sin and evil, and that in fact is how each has been told many a time in the past. But more negative readings are of course possible. The English Henry II was one of our better kings, and the reform of the civil law one of his major achievements. Indifferent to how people regarded him, he dressed simply and without all the pomp and external ostentation that characterized Becket. Should perhaps Becket not have at least compromised, rather than insisting on defending all the privileges of the Church up to the hilt? Again, though Hildebrand's achievements were considerable in forging the medieval papacy, and almost all of Europe was on his side in his first confrontation with the emperor, he went too far in trying to depose Henry IV a second time and died in exile at Salerno in southern Italy. Then again with Ambrose it would be wrong to conceal his other more dubious triumph over Theodosius two years earlier, when he had badgered the emperor into rescinding all punishment and compensation that might have been due from Christians at Callinicum, a small town on the Euphrates. In a burst of religious zeal they had burnt down the local synagogue and a chapel belonging to a heretical group of Gnostic Christians.

Today we live in an age of cynicism about those in power. Whether the issue be domestic or international, Christians have often been quick to condemn those in authority, speaking of narrow, self-interested motives holding the day. It is an easy judgement for a church to make, when it no longer has the position of power that it once did. But does this make its analysis any more plausible? Does not most human action proceed from mixed motives? And, if so, ought we not to extend greater sympathy to those earlier figures, who had such power and were called on to make difficult decisions?

Becket's vision was certainly a limited one, but he did at least try hard. Even before he became archbishop, as chancellor his personal life was beyond reproach and there is no doubt about the sincerity with which he approached his new calling. Then, however inadequately he had lived, in death his shrine stood as a constant reassurance to the oppressed that no princely power was absolute. Indeed, it is surely not without significance that it was a king with absolutist ambitions who ordered the shrine's destruction in 1538 – the tyrannical Henry VIII. Likewise, despite his commitment to a quite different approach, it was Gregory VII's reforms that brought about a rebirth of idealism in the Church which eventually blossomed in quite a number of unexpected ways, not least in the new religious orders of Francis and Dominic.

But what of Ambrose? In assessing his character, can his integrity over the massacre at Thessalonica really be allowed to outweigh his behaviour over Callinicum? Or should we blame him for all the Jew-baiting that Christians were to engage in over subsequent centuries? Though Ambrose, unlike his protégé Augustine of Hippo, was fluent in Greek and thus more widely read, he was still very much a creature of his time. He shared the traditional old Roman family prejudice not only against the Jews but also against all foreigners. He ridiculed, for instance, the Goths who were now streaming into the Empire, even when they had adopted Christianity. He would have nothing to do with their strange manner of dress and behaviour. But with this endorsement of conventional prejudices of the time, there also went a real willingness to identify with the ordinary religious values of his people. Elected bishop at the age of thirty-five by popular acclaim, much of his ministry suggests a bishop eager to further his people's faith by fully entering into its spirit. His writings were overwhelmingly pastoral in orientation, and such innovations as he did make were resolutely practical, such as his introduction of antiphonal chanting of the psalms and the singing of metrical hymns.

Callinicum of course shows the obvious danger in such close identification. But does not the Church of our own day equally err, in going to the other extreme? Contemporary Christianity often seems dominated by the language of 'empowering others' (marginalized groups of various kinds), and this is often presented as an alternative to the imposition of power, something we allegedly no longer do. But whether we think of State or Church, the language of democracy and consultation remains quite different from the reality. It is often precisely those who make most pretence of consultation who wield power most deviously. It is little wonder therefore that widespread cynicism has been the result. Ambrose, Hildebrand and Becket may sometimes have made the wrong decisions, but at least they did not conceal from themselves the reality of the responsibility they bore for good and for evil. We live in a very different world, but the ambiguities of power remain. Hildebrand was a good man and, had fortune shone on him, he too might have been canonized like Ambrose and Becket. Of course, like all of us, all three were imperfect: but they had a realism and honesty about power that today's world badly needs to recover.

14

Catherine of Siena

A young woman reforming the Church

Those who get too easily depressed by the current state of the Church – whether it be because of its disunity, some particular scandal or simply a general lack of confidence – do really need to take the Church's actual history with a bit more seriousness. For there never has been a golden age. Beset as we are by sin, inevitably each age has had its own characteristic set of problems, and often much worse than our own. The more interesting question therefore is not how things go wrong – they always do – but what means God employs to bring either the Church as a whole or particular individuals out of that mess. The Church was in one such big mess in the fourteenth century; it is how the situation was redeemed that still has something to teach us today.

The fourteenth century opens with two powerful monarchs locked in deadly combat: Philip IV of France and Pope Boniface VIII. The Pope not only resisted all attempts of Philip to impose taxation among his clergy but had also issued a papal bull, *Unam Sanctam*, in which he claimed for the papacy absolute authority in temporal as much as in spiritual matters. He even went so far as to declare that there could be no salvation except through such subjugation to Rome. Philip's response was to authorize the Pope's capture and imprisonment, and Boniface died not long after, broken in body and spirit. Philip, however, was determined that the papacy should never again prove such a difficult foe, and so secured the election of a Frenchman as pope, Clement V, who agreed to base himself at Avignon, papal territory in southern France, where it would be easy to keep the papacy subservient to French interests. So began the period of the Church's history which the poet Petrach was to dub its 'Babylonian captivity'. Not that all the Avignon popes were wicked men: some, like Benedict XII, tried to act responsibly, and he himself led a life of great devotion and austerity; but it remained a standing reproach to the Church that its leadership was now effectively in the pocket of one particular nation state – France.

It was into this world that a female saint was born, who was to have a decisive influence on the future direction of the Church. Inevitably, in the past men have been much better at securing the canonization of members of their own sex, but this particular saint provides one of many reminders that could be quoted which indicate how much the Church's history owes to women. Catherine of Siena was dead by the age of thirty-three, but one of the principal aims of her short life was to end this scandal of the Church being in the pocket of one particular nation. And for a young woman without any official status whatsoever, she acted in a quite extraordinary manner, cajoling those in power to a better way both through personal presence and by letter. These letters survive, and one thing they certainly do not show is any sense of deference to those in power. For instance, to Queen Joanna of Naples she writes: 'You will have to account to God for the souls that are perishing because of you. What account can you give? A very bad one.'[25] Or again, to the English mercenary John Hawkwood, whose splendid tomb survives in the cathedral at Florence, she remarks: 'It would be a fine thing if you would withdraw a little into yourself and reflect on all the trials and hardships you have had to endure in the Devil's pay and service.' But it was upon the weak-willed Pope Gregory XI that she was to have most impact, in persuading him to move the papacy back to Rome in 1377, only three years before her own death. To him she does not hesitate to write: 'I desire to see you a real man . . . For this reason, my soul's desire is for God, in his infinite mercy, to take all disordered affection and lukewarmness out of your heart and make a new man of you.'

What enabled her to get away with such forthrightness of speech? In a word, she was a saint. She spoke with authority that was born out of total dedication to God. Born the twenty-third out of her parents' twenty-five children, she resolutely refused to follow either of the two paths that were assumed for female children of her day: marriage or the enclosed life of a nunnery. Instead, by joining a loose association called the Third Order of Saint Dominic, she was able to anticipate by several centuries the life of nuns active in the world, with which we are of course so familiar today. In other ways – like all of us – she remained a creature of her time: for instance in her support of a new crusade against Islam, or in the horrifying austerities to which she made her body subject.

But with all these limitations went an overwhelming conviction of the love of God, something that emerges with particular clarity in her *Dialogue*, the account she has left us of her conversations with God the Father. It was because he was 'drunk with love', she writes, that God sent his Son to be a bridge across which we could pass in safety to his bosom. It is a work full of such powerful images. This is what she hears Christ say of communion: 'Just as the fish is in the sea and the sea in the fish, so am I in the soul that receives the bread and that soul in me, a sea of peace.'[26] But it is a relationship already grounded in the creation itself. When she hears God say, 'You are she who is not, I am he who is,' it is important to observe that what is being asserted is something positive, not something negative about ourselves: that it is only in God our creator that we truly live and have our being. Indeed, a true love of self can only benefit others, she argues, because we are all part of the one vineyard, and so enriching the soil in one part will eventually enrich it all.

Yet Catherine was to die thinking her life's mission a failure. For, though the papacy was now firmly established once more in Rome, the vacillating Gregory XI died shortly after his return to Rome, and in his place was elected a cruel, petty despot who was almost certainly mentally unstable, Urban VI. The cardinals discovered their mistake too late; a rival pope was elected for Avignon, and so began the period of church history known as the Great Schism. All of Europe divided in its choice of who was to be recognized as the legitimate pope, with England and Scotland, for instance, taking opposing sides. It took forty years before the dispute was finally resolved through the work of the Council of Constance (1414–18).

Catherine was to know none of this, living to see only the very beginnings of Urban's reign. She appears to give him unqualified endorsement, upbraiding the French bishops for their lack of support. However, in her defence it should be noted that this was long before Urban began his reign of terror, during which he even tortured and executed some of his own cardinals. Even so, there are signs of her trying to keep him on the straight and narrow. Admittedly, gone is the frank language that she had used with his predecessor; gone too the obvious affection she had for the earlier pope, despite his weaknesses, so clearly indicated by her favourite form of address for Gregory – 'sweetest daddy of mine'. Instead, she carefully tempers her language for this new, prickly pontiff. 'Pardon my presumption', she writes, when offering advice, only very indirectly hinting that his walking barefoot in procession had been one of his few acts so far to which she would be able to give unqualified approval.

Sadly, Urban proved beyond correction – unlike many of her other correspondents, most notably of course Urban's predecessor, Gregory. Why did they listen? It was because of her transparent goodness, the way in which she was so obviously afire with the love of God. Frank upbraiding there was, but it came out of love, love for that person, the longing to make them more fully part of God's love for the world. Most of her letters end: 'Abide in the sweet and holy love of God. Sweet Jesus. Jesus, Love'. They listened because her advice and urgings to do better came not out of any sense of superiority – her letters fully acknowledge her own failings – but out of an overwhelming conviction of sharing God's compassion for the world.

And is our own day really any different? Do not we as individuals and the Church as a whole need our Catherines – men and women who out of love can help us identify our faults and thus help us to do better? We live in an age in which love and friendship are thought to require constant praise and affirmation. But, if even those closest to us fail to help us identify our real selves, what hope do we have? Of course, rows may well be the result – none of us likes to hear the dirt on ourselves, but once the dust is settled, is that not one of the most obvious ways in which we as adults can continue to grow as human beings? Nor should we think that such advice can come only from those of the same gender. Part of Catherine's power lay precisely in her ability to critique men in such a non-threatening way that they were able to hear and act on her advice. We also need to listen, to male and female friends alike. Then we too can, like Catherine, be caught up into the life of that God she knew so well, a God who is 'drunk with love'.

15

Thomas Arundel

The saint who burnt heretics

'God struck him dumb; he was unable to speak or swallow for days before his death; and all a judgement upon him for having tied up the word of God in the mouths of the preachers.' 'A saintly man, a Christian candle in the darkness of the world, who even in death remembered to share that light with his friends.'[27] These two quotations well illustrate how easy it is to come to diverse conclusions about the same life, in this case that of Thomas Arundel, Archbishop of Canterbury from 1396 to 1414. In his case, he was in fact never canonized, but many who have behaved similarly in persecuting heretics were. If St Dominic (d. 1221) as the founder of the Dominican order sought to combat the Albigensian heresy in southern France by preaching and example, it was not long before his order had recruits such as St Peter Martyr (d. 1252), who was assassinated for his zeal as an inquisitor. But Arundel is a better example for us to take here, as it was he who introduced the practice of actually burning heretics into England.

If we ask why there could be two such radically different estimates of Arundel's career, the answer may briefly be given: his life was highly controversial in at least two respects. First, having served one king (Richard II) as chancellor and archbishop, he then played a leading part in his downfall and thus secured a continuing role for himself under Richard's successor, Henry IV. But, second and still more controversially – and here we come to the point of the first judgement upon him with which I began – he was a persecutor of the followers of the reformer Wyclif, the group known as the Lollards, indeed so much so that he earned for himself the title 'Hammer of the heretics'.

That said, it now becomes clear why his name is seldom now mentioned in church circles, far less as that of a saint. Rightly so, the reader may well reply. After all who in their right mind would wish to be associated with such an obvious political time-server, far less someone who was responsible for the burning of heretics, especially heretics who in some senses anticipated the Reformation? But is the issue that simple? One of the great advantages of studying history is that through attempting to understand times and cultures very different from our own those times and cultures can then in turn throw up a reflecting glass, a challenge, to our own life and times. Arundel seems to me to offer precisely such a challenge in one crucial area, that of the approach of society in general to the question of tolerance. This is, however, best approached indirectly by first looking at Arundel's political actions, about which it is indeed all too easy to be cynical.

Born into a wealthy noble family, his father, the Earl of Arundel, may well have marked out this, his third son, for the Church from birth. Certainly wealth and power played their part in securing rapid preferment. Such was the family's influence that by papal bull Thomas was made Bishop of Ely at the astonishingly early age of twenty. An inauspicious start one might have thought: for, though not uncommon, almost inevitably power at such an age generates corruption of mind and heart. But not so in the case of Arundel. By lucky chance quite a lot of historical evidence survives from Arundel's time at Ely, from which his modern biographer, Margaret Aston, is able to conclude that he was able and conscientious in his administration of the diocese.

So conscientious indeed that he seemed the obvious man to be made Chancellor of England at the age of thirty-three in 1386 to the young, volatile king, Richard II. Arundel served him well until 1397, when for some reason the mood of Richard changed towards him. There is some indication to suggest that it may have been partly due to Arundel's protests against the king's extravagances. At all events, despite having been made Archbishop of Canterbury the previous year, he was sentenced to banishment, only to return two years later as part of the future Henry IV's rebellion, and it was he who crowned the new king, going on to serve him in turn as chancellor.

From all this it would be very easy to deduce a time-server and opportunist. But such evidence as we have suggests a very different reading, that of someone trying to secure the best that he can for his country from a mercurial monarch. At his best Richard was capable of governing well, but there was also a vicious, spendthrift and tyrannical streak which finally decisively asserted itself in 1397, with Arundel inadvertently as a result sending his own brother to his death at the hands of Richard. There is some evidence to suggest that Richard was mentally unbalanced. So it is intriguing to observe that, in justifying his subsequent support for Henry, Arundel in a sermon before parliament directly compares himself with the prophet Samuel, who was also summoned by God to seek a substitute for a deranged king (Saul). However, ever the diplomat, Arundel allows Richard the fiction of having abdicated voluntarily; and so, rather than referring to Samuel's choice of David, the text he actually uses comes from Samuel's choice of Saul: 'Here is the man to rule over my people' (I Sam. 9–17). This seems rather more than just diplomatic sleight of hand. Arundel, I suggest, was trying to do the best for his country in difficult circumstances. Having failed with an unstable king, he looks elsewhere, but even then he avoids revelling in his old master's defeat.

Even readers who have sympathetically followed my argument thus far may still baulk at the fact that I wish to go further. For surely, it will be said, nothing could possibly be said in favour of Arundel the persecutor, especially given his decisive role in intensifying such persecution. For, though Gregory IX had founded the Inquisition in 1232, it was only with Arundel's

De haeretico comburendo of 1401 that the burning of heretics finally arrived in England. Now I hasten to say that I do not for a moment wish to defend such conduct. But to give Arundel a fair hearing we really do need to exercise our historical imagination, to think ourselves back into fifteenth-century England. In our own day we do not think it improper that those of us who are taxpayers are compelled to pay large sums to ensure our physical health, nor that those who might damage that health are prevented by law from publicizing their wares (e.g. drugs) or else are inhibited in the types of publicity they may use (as with tobacco). Well, think yourself back into a world where spiritual health was taken with equal seriousness. It was an age in which the Church was as much accepted as essential to society as the Health Service is to our own. Heretics were seen as just as dangerous to society's health as we now regard drug pushers as being (and note that many countries even to this day still impose the death penalty on the latter).

But even making all these historical allowances, can we really admire such a man? I venture to suggest that we can. Of course, what he did was wrong, but the more one investigates his life, the more one realizes that he did what he did for compassionate and honourable motives and in a compassionate and honourable way. So, for instance, the law itself allowed forty days for the handing over of the now forbidden books without any penalty accruing, and even in the case of the recalcitrant, Arundel himself made considerable efforts by patient argument (not torture) to try to ensure their conversion. This emerges with particular clarity from the personal account of his trial given by one of the Lollards himself, William Thorpe; and indeed only in two cases during Arundel's episcopacy were the offenders so obdurate that the death penalty was finally exacted.

But can such a life really have anything to teach us? Has it anything of that model of tolerant compassion that we would all now want to espouse? My suspicion is that, surprising as it may seem, Arundel may well have had a more generous understanding of tolerance than what often passes for the name in the modern world. Take the Salman Rushdie affair. All that most people in Britain detected in that business was the obvious intolerance on the part of Muslims in supporting the *fatwa* (or death sentence) on the author for criticizing Mohammad in his novel. What was seldom observed was the intolerance of Rushdie himself – or for that matter of most of the British public – in the way in which they condemned their Muslim fellow-citizens.

For think what Rushdie was attempting to do in *The Satanic Verses*. It was an attempt to parody, to lampoon, to render despicable all that Muslims hold most dear, in particular the sanctity of Mohammad. He was portrayed as naïvely endorsing a local polytheistic cult. The aim was clearly to hurt and to offend; not in any sense to win Muslims through compassion, far less argument, to what Rushdie at that time believed to be the truth. So what our own society was defending was in effect the right to be cruel, the right to be hurtful. Does that really give us such a strong moral advantage over Arundel? And what of the British public generally? Almost everyone, with the media in the lead, condemned Islam *en masse* without even taking the trouble to inquire what range of attitudes actually existed among Muslims in Britain. The truth in fact was that there were major differences of view, depending, for instance, on whether the Muslims were Barilwis or Deodandis, or Ahmadis or Maududis, to mention only two major contrasts. If such contrasts reflect Britain's Muslim community's origins in the Indian sub-continent, equally if one casts the net wider, it is important to note that al-Qaida draws its inspiration from the Saudi Wahhabi sect, and their views are far from typical of Arab belief in general. So, once more, where does that give us the advantage over Arundel, who at least took seriously the beliefs of those with whom he disagreed?

In none of this am I advocating a return to censorship. But such reflections do raise in my mind the question of whether it is really that obvious that modern tolerance, which often amounts just to cruelty or indifference, is really so incontestably morally superior to that earlier age. However puzzling it may be to us now, persecution was sometimes genuinely based on loving concern. Of course, torture and cruelty were also sometimes the consequence. But indifference too can have such results. Arundel at least got part of the way, taking the other seriously and valuing him in his own right. Indifference does not even guarantee that much. So, have we really progressed?

Part III: Reformation and Counter-Reformation

16

Thomas Cranmer

A hand for friendship and for fire

How can attendance at church possibly compete with the enticing headlines of Sunday tabloids spread out on the breakfast table or else on the bed? We can but try. What about this for a start: 'Kinky king cuckolded by curvaceous Kate,' or this: 'Archbishop's secret mistress found hidden in trunk.' Had our present newspapers and their style existed in the sixteenth century, such might have been the headlines in 1540 and 1543 respectively. And the details? Here is how the first few sentences about the king might have run: 'We told you it would go wrong – four-times-married King Harry taking on nineteen-year-old Catherine Howard, and him thirty years older. Well, Ann Boleyn did the dirty on him behind his back, and now within six months Harry has found Kate doing the same. But can you blame the young thing wanting a bit on the side with King Harry so overweight and his legs oozing puss all the time from his ulcers – and we know where he got those from (don't we?) with all that randy living!' In the case of the Archbishop one might have read something like this: 'Today a major fire at the Archbishop's Palace at Canterbury has shocked the nation – not because of the fire, but because of the horrendous double-life which it revealed our archbishop to be living. It is only four years ago that it became punishable by death for a priest to have a wife, and yet what should be smuggled out of the palace in a trunk but this saucy prelate's so-called very own wife – a German Margaret whom he claims to have married eleven years ago. At least we now know where all that nasty, new religion that this self-seeking hypocrite is imposing upon us is coming from – the Kraut in his bed'.

Such is how our contemporary press might have treated the two leading figures at the start of the English Reformation, Henry VIII and Thomas Cranmer. And of course there is no shortage of further tales that they could have added. Six-times-married Henry ended his autocratic reign at the age of fifty-five in January 1547. Cranmer was to survive another decade, through the triumph of his two Prayer Books of 1549 and 1552 under Henry's son, the sickly Edward VI, only to be finally burnt as a heretic under Henry's Catholic daughter, Mary, in 1556. And here once more our press could have had a field day. Cranmer, as we all know, unlike Bishops Latimer and Ridley, recanted no less than five times in what might most naturally be read as the last, desperate struggle of a coward to escape the inevitable fire.

Not an edifying tale, one might think, and hardly an auspicious beginning to the Reformation in England. Yet Roman practice at that time was scarcely any better. The beginning of the century had seen the licentious Borgia pope, Alexander VI, and in Julius II one even prepared to do battle in full armour. But, even if we confine ourselves to those in power while Cranmer was archbishop, the situation was not much of an improvement. For, although Paul III and Julius III were to take the first hesitant steps towards reform of the Church, both were tainted by scandal. The former had at least four illegitimate children. The latter was to become infatuated with a fifteen-year-old youth, Innocenzo, whom he had picked up on the streets of Parma. But such exchange of abuse and counter-abuse scarcely takes us very far. Both sides had their faults. What we surely need to do as Christians is learn from the past, not act like some modern journalists who simply muckrake in order to destroy reputations.

Take Cranmer first. Certainly, John Foxe, writing slightly later under Henry's other daughter Elizabeth, erred badly when he sought in his influential *Book of Martyrs* to make Cranmer out as the true St Thomas of Canterbury in place of Becket. Cranmer had none of the willpower or strength of determination needed to be the other man. Yet Foxe was right to this extent, that there does remain another side to be told. Even as archbishop Cranmer sought to live a disciplined life of prayer and scholarship, rising, for example, at five each morning. Reluctantly plucked from his study at Cambridge to help with Henry's first divorce, as well as loyal service to his new master, truth and compassion continued to be part of his motivation. Thus we know him to have interceded with Henry (sometimes successfully, sometimes not) for the lives of people of varied backgrounds and positions, for example for Fisher and More, for Ann Boleyn and the Princess Mary, for Thomas Cromwell and Bishop Tunstall. Even if he was not always successful in this – or indeed in his religious policy for that matter – he did at least succeed in making the royal court a gentler place than it might otherwise have been. It is true that, unlike his brief but public first marriage which had ended tragically with his wife dying in childbirth, his second was kept secret for more than a decade. Yet this was done for much of the time with the open connivance of the king, and that despite Henry's support in general for clerical celibacy. Margaret was the niece of a prominent Lutheran reformer, Osiander, and Cranmer had married her shortly before he became archbishop in 1532. Although the story of the trunk is a good tale, it was a false elaboration of the kind that characterizes quite a few of the yarns in today's newspapers. Cranmer had been anxious to save 'his treasure' in the trunk, but almost certainly what he intended by that remark were his manuscripts and not his wife! In any case she was to survive him, and marry twice more.

What she thought of her husband's prevarications at the stake we do not know. Of one thing, however, we can be certain. Cranmer's hesitations had little to do with fear, and everything to do with theology. Perhaps spurred on by his awareness of the disastrous consequences of religious conflict in Germany, like Henry he held a very high doctrine of the divine providential ordering of the world: that it was God and not human beings who made and unmade monarchs, and it was the subject's duty therefore to obey them. His final thrusting of his hand into the flames was a belated recognition that civil and divine obedience could not always march hand in hand.

The hand that was to be thrust into the flames was the same hand which Henry had requested on his own death-bed. Cranmer became progressively more and more Protestant as the years advanced. Indeed, it is often said that, had the flames not engulfed him, there would have been a third and much more Protestant Prayer Book. Henry was a different man. Whatever the truth about his lusts and his temper, he certainly believed in the old Catholic faith. To this day, British coins bear the legend 'F. D.' (*Fidei Defensor* or 'Defender of the Faith'), a title conferred on Henry by the Pope for his tract of 1521 in defence of seven sacraments rather than two, written in response to Luther and late in his reign while he was still trying to reassert Catholic orthodoxy. Removal of papal authority was one thing; change of belief quite another. Yet it was not for an orthodox priest that Henry asked on his death-bed, but for his old friend, Cranmer. When that old friend asked him for some sign that he put his faith in Christ, it was the hand that was to be burned that 'he did ring in his as hard as he could'. Henry certainly had his lusts, but once his conviction of the necessity for a male heir and his deep love for Jane Seymour are taken into account what emerges is a more complex and more engaging figure. Even the ulcers were probably not the result of syphilis, but of varicose veins.

Yet that more complex picture of Henry and Cranmer that I have tried to convey was not just true of them. It is the story of each and every one of us. As individuals each one of us is a mixture of good and bad, capable of great goodness and of great wickedness. We need efforts of imagination to understand one another, just as we need efforts of imagination to understand Henry and Cranmer – Cranmer's prevarications, caused by what seems now to us an absurd over-confidence in God's ordering of the state, Henry's apparent lusts, caused by his obsession with securing a male heir. That complexity, that imagination, is something our modern press and its readers too commonly fail to grasp. With them there is only the desire to pull down, to reassure that others also share in their readers' mediocrity.

But Christianity calls us to a very different vision. The hands that unite Catholic Henry and Protestant Cranmer tell of the need for us to be at once generous in our assessment of others and harsh in our judgement of ourselves. Like Cranmer, now is the time to face the fire that can both increase our charity towards those with whom we disagree and reveal to each one of us who we really are. In that light, as we shall see more clearly in subsequent chapters, neither Reformation nor Counter-Reformation can be deemed to hold the ultimate truth. Both alike had their faults, in theology and individual leaders alike. Conspicuous saint and sinner are to be found on both sides, and we shall learn by going beyond the limitations of both sides, as well by addressing similar limitations in ourselves.

17

Charles V and Nicholas Ferrar

The Emperor changes his clothes

To date, I have known four academics who committed suicide. In each case the problem was frustrated ambition and a sense of failure – though to any impartial, outside observer they could only have been regarded as very much above the average, run-of-the-mill don. In others, such frustrated ambition has taken the form of bitterness and bitchiness towards their colleagues, often souring their relationships with others. The academic world is of course by no means unique in this. Whatever the reader's occupation, other cases will probably easily come to mind: and, if we are ruthlessly honest, we may even see something of this in ourselves. People become so obsessed with one particular standard or measure of worth that it begins to eat away at their very souls.

The twentieth century witnessed the horrific results of megalomaniac ambitions in the lives of Hitler and Stalin, already anticipated to a high degree in the nineteenth century by the obsessions of Napoleon. All three ruled over large empires. Between the fall of the Roman Empire and Napoleon, the only comparable figure is the Holy Roman Emperor, Charles V, who offers us a very different tale. Born in Ghent in 1500, either by inheritance or by conquest he was to become ruler of what today we know as Holland, Belgium, Spain, Germany, Italy, Austria, Hungary, the Czech Republic and parts of Poland, as well as the Spanish territories in South

America and north Africa. But in no sense did he treat all this as his personal fief, as simply a tool for further self-advancement. Even when he had defeated the French king, Francis I, or the pope, Clement VII, he refused to impose humiliating conditions upon them, although he could easily have done so.

Indeed, it is arguable that all his wars were essentially defensive, and motivated by an ideal which in this respect at least makes him an engagingly modern character. Fluent in Flemish, Spanish, Italian and French, he was entirely free of the narrow nationalism already gripping England and France, which was so to convulse Europe in the centuries to come, and from which our own age is now seeking release through institutions like the European Union. A similar ideal motivated his religious policy. Only twenty-one when he met Luther at the Diet of Worms, he consistently sought reconciliation between Protestant and Catholic; fully alive to the corruptions of the contemporary Catholic Church, again and again he sought to influence the papacy towards summoning a universal council of the Church to correct abuses. But the papacy resisted, and he was only finally successful more than twenty years after Worms, when the Council of Trent began its work in 1545. Admittedly, as death approached he grew more hostile to Protestants, but historians often put this down more to pessimism and gout than as an indication of his real mind. Certainly, during his reign he both honoured his promise of safe conduct for Luther and later explicitly forbade the desecration of his tomb.

What motivated Charles in all of this is not in doubt: it was a religious vision. He saw himself at every moment as under the judgement of God, and that is what made possible his abdication in 1555. Power and ambition were firmly not absolutes for him. So the tears that were shed by the assembled nobles were genuine, as Charles made his abdication speech in Brussels. He then retired to a small house especially built for him within the grounds of a monastery in a remote country district of Spain, at Yuste. There he enjoyed the singing of the offices of which he was so fond, surrounded by a few paintings of his favourite artist, Titian.

Now jump a century to seventeenth-century England. Like his father, Nicholas Ferrar had been active in business, working on behalf of the Virginia Company and its concerns in the American colonies. He even became a Member of Parliament to further its interests. But when James I took the company under government control, an incentive was provided for him to rethink his life. Together with thirty or so members of his family, in 1625 he retired to Little Gidding, a farmstead about eighteen miles from Cambridge. There the small community adopted a regular pattern of worship and prayer: a major service at ten every morning, short meditations on the hour and a rota for ensuring that the entire Psalter was read each day. Among those who constituted what was called 'the little Academy', time was also set apart for discussion on specific themes. The records of some of these conversations survive, and one of the most long and interesting is devoted to that very figure with whom I began, Charles V.[28]

On the surface this was not an obvious choice, but Charles and Nicholas had in fact much in common. In particular, both exhibited a largeness of vision uncommon among their contemporaries. As a young man Ferrar had travelled in Europe, and certainly was no 'little Englander'. His community read widely from continental literature. Before the age of twenty Nicholas' nephew had already translated the gospels into twenty-four languages. Unusual for the time, the community's reading also included Roman Catholic devotional writings, perhaps the most familiar to us today being those of St Francis de Sales. Indeed, it is quite likely that Ferrar's decision to found such a community without perpetual vows was itself modelled on the recently founded Oratorians, whose most famous recruit would in due course be another Englishman, John Henry Newman. Devotional tracts on Charles V were also commonplace in the Belgium of the time, and so their decision to consider Charles' life at length once more has a continental, a larger inspiration.

But there was of course a deeper motive, to be seen in those conversations to which I have already alluded. As Ferrar observes: 'That as all things of this world are ... nothing in themselves, nor have we the propriety of them ... this is that, which Charles, as it were, under his royal seal by his so often represented surrender hath verified unto us.' In other words, for Nicholas the example of Charles is one of worldly ambition put firmly in its place. Their common retreat expresses more fully what had already motivated both their lives in the world: the desire to gain freedom from the kind of application of our desires and ambitions which can so easily destroy us. It is this ability to use the past to liberate and not enslave us that (among other things) T. S. Eliot celebrates in 'Little Gidding', one of his *Four Quartets*.[29]

Certainly, the result was emphatically not escapism. Charles continued to be consulted by his dutiful son, Philip II, who even built another monastery for the same order as part of his own royal palace, the Escorial near Madrid. On a more local level, Nicholas not only took responsibility for the education of the children of the district, he was also sought out for advice by a regular stream of visitors, including Charles I. It is also to Ferrar that we owe the publication in 1633 of the collection of George Herbert's poetry known as *The Temple*. Nor were either of their two communities idyllic places of peace. Charles was frequently infuriated by the excessive deference of the monks; Nicholas by the unrelenting hostility of his sister-in-law, Bathsheba. Yet each deepened the lesson that they had learnt in their worldly life, that all our ambitions, all our longings must stand under divine judgement, and be relativized by the absolute values of our religion: it is only that way we can gain true freedom, true content, whether we live in the world or in the cloister.

And so what of ourselves? Do Charles and Nicholas not summon us also to retreat, not necessarily to the permanent retreat of the cloister but certainly to a periodic standing back from ourselves, from our ambitions, from our deepest desires? We too need to hear the whisper of God in the silence of our hearts, giving us a sense of proportion and with it a sense of peace. What a difference a few moments of silence each day could make, or a few days joining with monks or nuns on a retreat in the peace of their cloister. Then, even when there comes that deafening clamour of what sounds like failure or defeat, we will still be strong enough to stand our ground. The still small voice, the divine whisper that hints of another system of values, will have silenced the thunder in our hearts. There will be no temptation to take our life, no temptation to bitterness. There will only be the thought of the love with which both men died: Nicholas 'singing' of the heavenly banquet, Charles chanting 'Jesus' as he clutched his beloved wife's crucifix to his breast.

18

Teresa of Avila

Transcending male and female, faith and works

Let me begin with two memories from my past. It was a beautiful spring day on which the minibus climbed up the tortuous road from the city of Haifa to the top of the mountain that lies behind this modern Israeli town. And at the top what a magnificent view! There amidst all the luxurious vegetation it was hard to envisage that here I was standing on the very spot – Mount Carmel – where Elijah challenged the prophets of Baal, and then slaughtered them (1 Kgs 18.17–40). Now for a younger David Brown trudging in the intense heat of a Spanish summer with a rucksack on his back, first the long distance from the railway station to the youth hostel, and then after only a short rest down, down the hill from the fortified city of Avila to the sandy, treeless plain below and the Convent of the Incarnation, where Teresa spent twenty-six years of her life (1536–62). One key moment in the life of this same Teresa was subsequently immortalized in a famous sculpture by Bernini at Rome, as she was sent into rapture by an angel who appeared to pierce her heart with his spear.[30]

Two very different images of the religious life: the male Elijah up the mountain actively seeking out and destroying God's enemies; the female Teresa down in the plain waiting passively to be pierced by the dart of divine love. In Christian history this has often been taken as exactly the right model for understanding the relation between the two sexes and their respective roles. But despite Teresa's best-known experience of God, that was emphatically not Teresa's own view. She summons male and female alike to be both active and passive (or receptive), and it is upon the implications of that summons that I want to reflect here.

Teresa was born into a society – sixteenth-century Spain – in which it was simply assumed that the female's role was a passive one, typified by Teresa's own calling as a nun. To understand her position, we must banish from our minds all modern images of nuns serving actively as teachers, nurses and so on. In Teresa's day the only option was to serve in an enclosed order. Even then the primary purpose of the convent was usually to pray for the repose of the dead (mostly men), those whose wealth had endowed the convent in the first place. So that was what was expected of her when she first joined the Convent of the Incarnation at Avila, a house belonging to the Carmelite order which claimed descent from Elijah and still to this day has a convent on Mount Carmel.

Admittedly, the expected passivity had its compensations. Teresa was given a suite of rooms that included even her own personal guest room for family and friends. But she will have none of this. Perhaps in part inspired by that very different image of Elijah, she rebels, and urges the total reform of the Carmelite order, male as well as female. Not only are the comforts to go, but the order is to seek independence from all those endowments. Their first aim should be closer identification with Christ, not prayers for the wealthy dead. And to achieve her goal, she does not hesitate to play off one party against another – now appealing to the city council, now to the bishop, now to the papal nuncio, now to the general of the order, now to the king himself. Nothing was going to stop her. If necessary (as at Toledo in 1569), she and her nuns worked by night to turn a couple of neighbouring domestic houses into a convent, knocking down the wall between them; that way she was able to present the authorities with a *fait accompli*. Sharing with Elijah Jewish blood, what in effect she does is subvert all those proud conventions of the Spanish nobility, purity of blood and the proper ordering of society that was alleged to go with it. A repeated theme is that we are all God's friends; so by implication all distinctions based on class are now abolished.

But, note, she is equally insistent that her reforms should not impose a fresh straitjacket, a new passivity upon her nuns. So, ironically, although the reformed version of her order is known as the Discalced Carmelites (literally Carmelites 'without sandals'), she tells her nuns that sandals may be worn whenever the weather or other circumstances require it. Again, she carried a bell and a drum about with her, for she thought dancing one of the best ways in which to express our natural joy in the Lord. Freedom and spontaneity were thus integral to her vision of the reform, and indeed one of her best-known remarks is the plea that 'God deliver us from sullen saints'.

Equally, she refuses to be bound by the conventions of education. As with women generally at that time, her own had been minimal. She knew almost no Latin. Indeed, she was so ignorant that in one of her writings she misidentifies a verse from one of the lesser creeds (the Athanasian) as part of a psalm. Yet despite such limitations and despite narrowly escaping condemnation from the Inquisition, she wrote several powerful works that reflect her view of prayer. These beautifully capture her vision of the Christian life as one that ought effectively to blend passivity and activity.

Teresa was born only two years before the date conventionally used to mark the beginning of the Reformation, when in 1517 Luther nailed his ninety-five theses on the door of the castle church at Wittenburg, challenging established views. It is easy to fall into the trap of supposing that this must be more than mere coincidence, that Teresa must therefore be counted as part of the Catholic reaction in the Counter-Reformation. But the truth is that Luther's preoccupations passed her by. In part no doubt because of her own ignorance, neither what Luther was reacting against nor the exchanges between him and his opponents find any clear echo in her writings. Instead, Teresa displays an extraordinary freedom in how she expressed herself. Not for her the traditional three stages of prayer – the purgative, the illuminative, and the unitive. Even her sevenfold distinction she hastily qualifies by saying that God approaches us in not a 'few' ways but in a 'million'.[31]

More importantly, the priority of grace over works, of divine action over ours, is as prominent in her writings as the most ardent Protestant could possibly wish. Yet this stress on receptivity to divine grace is combined with a repeated demand for action, for works to flow from the transforming power of divine grace. In her autobiography she tells us that we get it all wrong when we think something all our own work. Certainly, she admits, that is the way it will feel at first, so weighty do God's demands initially seem to fall upon us, but eventually our understanding will change. To use her own analogy: when we begin the life of prayer, at first we feel as though it is we who have to do all the work, carrying, as it were, all the buckets of water from the divine well. But, gradually, this becomes more like a system of conduits, then natural streams flowing into us, before finally grace bursts upon us as pure spontaneity like unexpected showers of rain from heaven.

Yet it is not that our own efforts will ever cease; it is just that we become more and more conscious of the divine part in them. To use another analogy from her writings, every human soul is a mansion with many rooms, and God is the precious jewel in the central room at the very heart and centre of our souls. Because, however, each room is separated from the next only by glass, it is very easy for us to think that we have arrived at the centre when we have not. Instead, we need always to be on our guard, particularly against more insidious forms of temptation, lest we mistake the intermediate for our final goal. So, for instance, she observes that often it is basically good people who are most quick to condemn faults in others. The result is that they put themselves at an even further remove from the forgiving Love that should have been their true centre.

A familiar gospel story tells of how the busy Martha was condemned while her sister, Mary, is praised, as she sits listening at Jesus' feet (Lk. 10.38–42). Such was Teresa's freedom that even here, with Scripture apparently endorsing an image for women contrary to her own, she will have none of it. Using the long-standing tradition which had identified this Mary with Mary Magdalene, she insists that Mary is really praised because she combined both receptive and active lives: for the woman who listens becomes also the woman who wiped Jesus' feet with her hair.[32]

Whatever one may think of her exegesis of the passage concerned, I am sure that she was right in her overall estimate. Whether male or female, we passively receive from God only in order to be empowered to act for our own transformation and that of the world. In words commonly attributed to her: 'Christ has no body now on earth but yours; no hands but yours, no feet but yours; yours are the feet with which he goes about doing good; yours are the hands with which he blesses people now.'[33] Would that we all could transcend Reformation disputes in the way Teresa did. Then we too would cease to be preoccupied by how active and receptive roles should be distributed between men and women. Instead, women and men alike would focus on being passive before God as a way of receiving the grace that can enable us to be truly active for him in his world, on being saints like Teresa.

19

John Cosin

Vain ceremonial or bodily worship

2 February 1628 was an eventful day in the history of Durham
Cathedral. A young and recently appointed canon had been
busy from two to four in the afternoon, climbing up ladders
and placing candles and wax torches here, there and everywhere, so that by the time of the evening service the cathedral
was a blaze of light, with over two hundred spread throughout
the cathedral, and sixty of them round the altar itself. Not only
that, the whole feel of the worship was markedly different from
what it had been a decade earlier. Among the changes introduced over the course of that period had come, in place of a
communion table placed lengthwise in the middle of the quire,
a stone altar located permanently against a magnificent Gothic
screen which had survived the Reformation (though now
bereft of all the numerous alabaster statues of saints that had
once adorned it). Again, rather than sitting throughout, people
were now expected to stand for the Creed and to kneel for
prayer and to receive communion. Music too had arrived in a
big way; gone were the metrical psalms and in their place had
come chanting and anthems. And the priests were splendidly
arrayed in copes.

It was not a change to everyone's taste, especially one of the
older canons, who had just turned sixty. A former headmaster
of the cathedral school, he thought he knew how to put these
new boys on the block, as it were, in their place, and launched a

ferocious counter-attack in a sermon later that year, on Sunday July 27th. It is fine stuff, fiery, caustic and telling in its rhetoric. It is worth quoting a brief sampler of how he describes the behaviour of this young upstart canon, little more than half his age: 'Our youthful Apollo repaireth the quire, and sets it out gaily with strange Babylonish ornaments; the hallowed priests dance about the altar, making pretty sport, and fine pastime, with trippings and turnings, and crossings and crouchings; while choristers and singing men shout and cry. Can these paltry toys bring to our memory Christ and his blood-shedding? Did Christ minister the sacrament in such a manner to his disciples at the last supper? Was there an altar in the chamber where he supped? Did Christ put on a cope laden with images, or did he change his garments?'

But Peter Smart's thirty years of experience in Durham were no match for the rising star of the new canon, John Cosin. For he had powerful allies behind him, not only the dean, Richard Hunt, and the bishop, Richard Neile, but also the king himself. The previous year Cosin had published at Charles I's request a book of prayers, his influential *Collection of Private Devotions*. So it is not Cosin who was reprimanded but Smart. He was charged with 'preaching a seditious sermon against the decent and allowed ceremonies of the Church of England'. Upon his refusal to pay the imposed fine, he was sent to prison in 1631, and there he languished for ten years until the politics of England changed once more.

Bishop Neile and Smart had been contemporaries at Westminster School, and to Smart Neile was a 'heavy headed lubber, put out of that school for a dunce and a drone'. But Neile had held seven bishoprics – 'the seven hills of Rome' is how Smart puts it – and thereby had been able to advance many sympathetic to his own views. Now, however, the most distinguished of them, William Laud, Archbishop of Canterbury, was in the Tower, and the process which led first to Laud's execution in 1645 and then to that of the king himself in 1649 had begun. So it was that on the verge of the Civil War, in 1641, Smart was at last freed by parliament and Cosin himself put on trial. Despite his best attempts to conceal much of what had happened, it was now Cosin who was punished by being deprived of his then Mastership of Peterhouse, Cambridge. Cosin spent the next twenty years in exile in France, before returning once more in triumph to Durham in 1660 as its new bishop. With him as the principal architect of the 1662 Prayer Book, the Church of England then began to take more closely the form in which we know it today.

But why all the fuss? Why candles at Candlemas, and such insistence upon ritual – 'trippings, and turnings and crossings'? In my last job I had a colleague who was a psychologist, one of whose main areas of research was body codes, what our postures either explicitly or implicitly convey. He turned up quite a few surprises, among them, for instance, a high empirical correlation between pulling up one's socks and the presence of sexual attraction!

One thing upon which Cosin was most insistent was the fact that as embodied creatures we cannot escape saying things about ourselves by our posture just as much as by what we say. In the sixteenth and seventeenth century, sitting was intended as a means of avoiding giving reverence to anything purely human. But the danger was that in refusing to employ any of the customary symbols of God's presence one might end up either with no sense of the presence of God at all, or else at best a split view of one's relationship to him, all head and no body. That is perhaps why Evangelical Christianity has had such a strong tradition of emotionally charged hymns: body or heart has to make its presence felt somewhere. But just as powerful can be kneeling at the altar rail, waiting expectantly to receive.

Certainly the biblical Candlemas, as described by Luke (2.22–40), was all about the body, about using tangible signs to express ourselves. The wealthy were expected to give a lamb, and the poor (like Mary) two pigeons to signify their thanksgiving to God for the child newly born. Simeon's response was to speak of the infant Christ as 'a light to lighten the Gentiles'. Stemming from that description, there began the medieval practice of festooning churches on this particular day with a blaze of light. Just as light can dispel the darkness and gloom of winter, so can Christ our Light now transform the darkness of our sins and the blackness of our fading hopes. Indeed so powerful was such symbolism in Scotland's even shorter winter days that its popularity succeeded in displacing Lady Day (the Annunciation, March 25th) as one of the quarter days that marked the agricultural year.

But of course symbolism can sometimes go badly wrong. Smart was surely right about that. Cosin too was not without his faults. But here at least he was clear. One of the changes to the Prayer Book which he failed to carry into effect was his plan to introduce as a central plank of the Catechism a reference to the need for each new church member to learn 'the outward reverence of my body'. 'Outward' alludes to the Catechism's definition of a sacrament ('outward and visible sign of an inward and spiritual grace'), and so, like sacrament, hints at inward transformation through grace. Almost certainly the Catholic wing of the Church of England would have been stronger today, had it kept alive such an equation between inward and outward, and not fought so often for correct ceremonial forms in and of themselves.

Cosin made no such mistake, as the ending of his life so beautifully illustrates. Throughout most of his adult life he was in acute pain from a kidney stone. Indeed, because of it in later life he seldom achieved more than two hours of sleep a night. During the day the pain was often so severe that he had to get out of his coach and be carried by sedan chair, in order to avoid further aggravation from the rougher parts of the road. But he refused to be embittered by his condition, and this is what characterizes his last moments. Now (15 January 1672) wearing a bandage tightly round his head to ease the pain, but feeling the end near, he asks to receive Holy Communion one last time. Unable to kneel, he kneels in the only way of which he is capable – by taking off his cap as it were, the bandage round his head that was easing his pain. And with the words, 'Lord, I bow the knees of my heart,' he dies.

Body and mind in perfect unison. Without that integration,

incense, candle, bowing and struttings are all alike without value. But with it, they can carry us, body and soul alike, into God's own greater future.

Part IV: The Modern World

20

Joseph Butler

Reason and nature as sacramental

Although born at Wantage near Oxford of parents of modest means, Joseph Butler was twice to be associated with the northern diocese of Durham, on both occasions with positions carrying great prestige and wealth. The second occasion was for the last two years of his life, when in 1750 he became Bishop of Durham. Three years earlier he had declined the offer of Canterbury, pleading poverty, despite a nephew's offer of a loan of £20,000. At least the palatine see of Durham presented no such problems, such was its intrinsic wealth! Nor had the earlier offer of the wealthy parish of Stanhope in Weardale, the valley of the River Wear in the south of the county, where he was rector for over fifteen years, from 1725 to 1740.

In refusing Canterbury, Butler gave as one of his reasons that 'it was too late to support a failing church'. Such a comment may seem to ratify Hutchinson's judgement upon him, in his 1785 *History of Durham*, that there was about Butler 'a natural cast of gloominess', and that this was reinforced by a quiet, rural village such as Stanhope, which was really 'too solitary for his disposition'. However, that would, I think, be quite the wrong reading of the situation. For there was in fact a great deal to be gloomy about in the eighteenth-century Church. On the one side, it was threatened by extreme rationalism in the movement known as deism, which insisted that all one needed to know about God could be known from the natural world without any reference to the Bible. On the other hand, equally problematic were those who responded by placing exclusive reliance on the Bible and denying any relevance of reason or nature to faith. It was the genius of Butler to insist that both factions were wrong, that Christianity is not only a reasonable faith but also one whose revelation builds upon what we already know about God from the world about us. The development of just such an argument reached fruition at Stanhope in 1736, in the publication of one of the two books for which he is best known, his *Analogy of Religion*.

Much of its argument is so bound up with eighteenth-century disputes that it is not easily accessible to the contemporary reader. Yet its central message most certainly is, which is that Christianity is both a reasonable faith and one which takes the world about it with utmost seriousness. Newman, writing a century later, identified Butler's perennial contribution in precisely these two aspects. By briefly focusing on each of them in turn, I hope to illustrate not only why this work of Butler's continues to remain of such fundamental importance but also the kind of impact such ideas had on Butler's life, and thus could possibly have on our own.

First, then, the question of the reasonableness of Christianity. The most quoted sentence from the *Analogy* is Butler's claim that 'probability is the very guide of life'. His point is that the Christian faith only seems unreasonable for so long as one operates with the wrong model of reason. Of course, if you want a logical, formal proof such as occurs in mathematics, you cannot have it. But very little of what we believe as we go about our daily life is like that; so why should we expect anything different of religion? Consider one of Butler's more domestic examples, the precise time of year at which one decides to put out bedding plants. That is hardly a matter of strict calculation. Much depends upon inference from past experience: how late, for instance, the frosts have been known to occur in one's particular part of the world and so forth. So similarly, then, with a whole range of other decisions in life, even momentous ones like whom one is going to marry, what career one is likely to pursue and so on. It is all a matter of weighing up probabilities, not strict certainties.

It is against this stress on the reasonableness of Christianity that one should set his hostility to John Wesley and his cult of what was known at the time as 'enthusiasm'. They met in 1739 when Butler was Bishop of Bristol. Butler declared to Wesley that his insistence upon fervour in religion was 'a horrid thing, sir, a very horrid thing'. He demanded that Wesley leave his diocese immediately: 'You have no business here; you are not commissioned to preach in the diocese; therefore I order you to go hence.' A somewhat severe exchange between two clergy of the Church of England, one might think. To understand the depth of Butler's hostility, one needs to appreciate the danger he detected lurking behind what was to become known as Methodism, a danger of retreat on the part of religion from reason. For Butler it was vital to insist that reason is an essential part of God's creation and not something of which religion should appear afraid, through urging retreat into the realm of private experience and emotion.

In one sense Wesley had the last laugh, since long after Butler was dead he had several successful missions in the Wear Valley, where Butler's one-time parish was located. On his first visit there he attracted a large crowd, though he preached at five in the morning. Later the room where he was speaking was so full that some of the floorboards collapsed. Fortunately, no one was hurt apart from a dog which had the misfortune to be under a window when a panicking man jumped out of it! The successful growth of 'enthusiasm' within Butler's erstwhile parish is well illustrated by the fact that in the late nineteenth century the Primitive Methodists found it necessary to build a chapel with a larger seating capacity than that of the parish church. So in one sense Wesley had clearly won.

Yet in another sense it is not implausible to claim that in the long run Anglicanism and Methodism both had lost out, since enthusiasm ceases to have much appeal once a climate is created in which Christianity is no longer seen as a reasonable or viable option. And so, what we need today is surely not a fresh choice between one or other, but a frank recognition that the Church needs both, both the reasonableness of Butler and the enthusiasm of Wesley.

One way Butler tried to demonstrate the reasonableness of religion was by drawing frequent analogies between the world of nature and the God revealed in the Bible: hence the title he chose for his book, *The Analogy of Religion*. To give but one example: if within nature caterpillars can be transformed into something as different as butterflies, is the claim of the Christian revelation really too hard to believe, of a similar dramatic transformation of ourselves after death? Newman speaks of having learnt from Butler's use of such illustrations that the world is really 'a sacramental system' with 'material phenomena as types or imitations of things unseen'.

In trying to understand the relevance of this second aspect of Butler's thought, it is perhaps easiest to start from the sense of sacrament with which readers will already be familiar. Church life at Stanhope was very different from what it is today. Communion would have been celebrated only five times a year. Butler did not increase their frequency, but he was concerned to secure a more reverential attitude. For instance, he built his own private oratory in the rectory while at Stanhope. Later, at Bristol he erected an elaborate marble cross in his private chapel there. Such actions were to lead to a pamphlet published after his death (in 1767) that accused him of being a covert Roman Catholic. There is not an iota of truth in this accusation. By contemporary standards he would have to be judged a very moderate, middle-of-the-road Anglican.

In all of this his concern was really for something much more fundamental than mere reverence for the eucharist. The sacrament itself was simply an important test case. In it ordinary things of the world, bread and wine, are used by God to point to something much deeper, to the creative transformation of ourselves, just as the pounding of the corn is made new as bread and the treading of the grape as wine. But, Butler asks, is all the world not like that, offering pointers to us, sacramental signs of something deeper, of a God at work in ourselves and the natural world and calling it (and us) to a greater destiny, the destiny that brings our world to complete fruition, a destiny disclosed in the Scriptures? In forming that vision, of a world of nature that points to God, it is surely not too fanciful to suppose that the lyrical beauty of the Weardale valley played an important part.

A reasonable faith and revelation completing our knowledge of a God whom we have already encountered in the beauty of nature: two fundamental marks of classical Anglicanism. Little wonder then that Newman describes Butler as 'the greatest name in the Anglican church'. That of itself scarcely makes him a saint. But it is an understanding of God's world that brought him close to God through nature and Bible alike, and helped foster the faith of countless others who followed him subsequently in his thinking.

21

John Wesley

Psychology and conversion

The New Testament is full of references to the need for conversion, and of descriptions of the impact of such experiences on people's lives. But should this be the model for all our lives, or only for those new to the faith? And, if for all, how exactly? One way of attempting to answer that question might be to consider a famous case of conversion such as that of John Wesley. An event momentous for the subsequent history of the Church, this took place on 24 May 1739. Listening to someone preaching on Luther's Preface to the Epistle to the Romans, Wesley felt his heart, he tells us, 'strangely warmed', as, putting his whole trust in Christ, he experienced the assured certainty of his sins being swept aside. The result – 40,000 sermons and 200,000 miles later – was the foundation of Methodism, shortly after Wesley's death, now one of the major Protestant denominations worldwide.

Although at the time Wesley had already been an ordained priest of the Church of England for ten years, and a conscientious and devout one at that, the initial interpretation he gave to that experience was as the inauguration of a true faith. He now knew what Luther's talk of justification by faith meant. He had been freed from a gospel of works through this experience of the liberation that God's free and gracious pardon brings to those who trust in Christ as their Lord. His brother Charles had undergone a similar experience a few days earlier, and he too saw their experience as decisive: something required of everyone if their faith were to be truly acknowledged as a reality. Indeed, so much was Charles convinced of such a universal necessity that when in 1740 his elderly mother, Susanna, spoke of experiencing a powerful sense of being released from sin as she received Holy Communion, he immediately interpreted her words in this light: that hitherto she had lived in 'a legal night of seventy years'. Susanna's response, however, was emphatically to reject Charles' interpretation of her life: 'I am not one of those who have never been enlightened . . . but have many years since been fully wakened'.[34]

The experience of the two brothers, as with all historical events, can of course be interpreted in several possible ways, some positive, some negative. One might, for instance, argue that the real cause of John's change of heart was the bitter disappointment he had just experienced as a missionary in Georgia. Not only had he failed to achieve any great success with either the settlers or the Indians, he had also had a series of embarrassing relationships with women, first on board ship then in the colony itself. Not that he had committed some gross sin, but he had at the very least behaved unwisely and immaturely. Similar problems had occurred earlier in his career at Oxford, where he had been a Fellow of Lincoln College. Even when he did marry (his bride was the widow Molly Vazeille), nothing could be clearer than that she was the wrong person for him. Almost certainly part of the reason for Wesley always being on the move was his desire to escape 'the ferret' at home. Indeed, the marriage was to end in separation, with his wife leaving for Newcastle, and Wesley making no attempt to bring her back.

More charitable readings of what lead up to the conversion are of course also possible. On the boat across the Atlantic he had met and admired some Moravian Christians, a pietistic sect now reinvigorated under the leadership of the wealthy German, Count Zinzendorf. Their simple faith – Zinzendorf reduced the content of Christianity to a single page – enabled them to show a confidence in the face of possible death which Wesley clearly envied. It seemed in such marked contrast to all the complexities of his own life. The nickname 'Methodist' had already been invented for the Holy Club which he had formed in Oxford. There had been worthy aims in abundance in his 'method', conscientious, simple rules for daily living – rising early, regularity in prayer, frequent communion (at least once a week), visiting the sick and prisoners and so forth, but it all seemed to lack the basic joy which the Moravians so obviously possessed.

But must we choose between such apparently competing explanations? Might not both contain a measure of truth, with God working as much through Wesley's defective psychology as through appeal to his heart and intellect? So far as psychology is concerned, the roots of the problem can be traced back much further, into his childhood. Of his two parents, one – his clerical father – was constantly in debt despite a good income, while it fell to the other – his mother Susanna – to try to keep the family flourishing through her own personal energy and self-discipline. In a rash moment Susanna admitted to John that 'your father and I seldom think alike'. Inevitably, parental tensions were to have their effect upon the children of the marriage. One daughter (Sukey) found herself compelled to flee her husband. Another (Hetty) gave birth to an illegitimate child. A third (Martha) ended up married to a worthless, adulterous cleric. Was there perhaps a desperate desire to escape the home, but insufficient preparation to ensure that the outcome was a happy one? Certainly, it would be easy to read John's failed romances in terms of a strong psychological need for a woman as powerful as his mother. Yet sadly, as we have seen, when such a personality did cross his path, it was the wrong woman for him. Equally, one might read his Oxford 'methodism' as an attempt to re-establish the positive elements of security that his mother had provided in that troubled home.

Whatever truth such amateur psychologizing holds – and it has been done by many before me – it would be foolish to suggest that this of itself undermines the religious value of either Wesley's pre- or post-conversion life. The 'method' of his early days did generate a life of real prayer and devotion. Its very intensity, however, also meant that something was missing. This the 1738 experience provided – a spontaneity and joy that now could be added to his practice of the Christian faith. Put that way, and one can now see God working in and through Wesley's psychological inheritance, and not against it.

And that is what I would suggest God does with each one of us. He works through the particularities of our individual psychologies, rather than requiring the same blueprint for all. This can be seen from Wesley's own career. Even as he listened to Luther on Romans, it was to a man with a different problem. For Wesley that experience of assurance came as an answer and corrective to a deep sense of failure in personal relationships. For Luther the primary focus was rather on the almost neurotic obsession with guilt and sin that his monastic career had hitherto created. Meanwhile, the great Moravian awakening that had taken place under Zinzendorf in 1727 was different again: unadulterated joy at the dissolving of tensions within the community.

Where our natural sympathies lie will vary from individual to individual. Some will be most attracted to Luther's experience of conversion, others to Wesley's, and yet others to Zinzendorf's. But for many what is required is something quite different – perhaps even the very reverse of what was needful in Wesley's case. So laid-back have some of us become that what is actually required is greater consciousness, not less, of the role of rules, a need to be shocked out of our self-satisfaction, and so made more open to God and to our fellow human beings. By contrast, perhaps for others what is most needful is an attack of barrenness in prayer, or failure in human relationships, for that can sometimes act as an impetus to humility and as a forceful reminder of the call to empathize with those less fortunate than ourselves. In short, there is no one answer, no one remedy that meets each individual's situation.

It is to Wesley's great credit that this is something which he himself came to see. Shortly before his conversion he had begun to question the faith of William Law, his erstwhile hero as a spiritual writer. However, by 1770 he could write that, although Law denied the necessity of such an experience of justification, his salvation was not in doubt. In 1779 he went further, arguing that 'no man is finally saved without works'. Instead, he now sought in his sermons to transcend all those Reformation arguments about faith versus works. Justification and sanctification (or the 'pursuit of perfection', as he preferred to call it) are both required, and neither should be exalted above the other. His final judgement on his conversion thus becomes not a move from unbelief to belief, but rather from the status of servant to that of son.

Zinzendorf, who had so shaped the pattern of simple Moravian belief that played such a major part in Wesley's great conversion experience, is sometimes claimed as the first ecumenist.[35] Certainly the first to use the word, in that unecumenical age he refused even to deny faith to the Pope himself. In our own day, do we not all need a similar charity and breadth of vision, when we consider the question of conversion? Each and every one of us stands in need of the grace of God, but we do not all need the same thing. Some of us need to discover trust; others their basic sinfulness; yet others a sense of gratitude. But all are aspects of conversion, the power of God's grace to re-make us, not in spite of what we are psychologically, but exactly through and in what we are. It is for that recreation that we need to pray. Wesley as an old man began to develop that larger vision; so must we.

22

Wilberforce, Newton and Simeon

Evangelical struggle for a larger vision

They were frightened, wondering what fate lay in store for them, snatched as they had been from their native West Africa to serve on the plantations of the West Indies. Conditions were cramped and, as was usual on such journeys, significant numbers would die. With sanitation at a minimum the smell of their own excrement fouled the air, and the odour often penetrated to the captain's cabin above. But his mind was elsewhere, deep in communion with God, writing of his own joy at having found the Lord. 'How sweet the name of Jesus sounds/ In a believer's ear!/ It soothes his sorrows, heals his wounds,/ And drives away his fear./ It makes the wounded spirit whole,/ And calms the troubled breast;/ 'Tis manna to the hungry soul,/ And to the weary rest.'

To us it is scarcely credible that so beautiful a hymn could have been written in such a context, with such a stark contrast between privilege and misery before the author's very eyes; still more remarkable that the contrast was allowed to stand by someone who had himself experienced the degradations of slavery. Yet this had indeed been the author's own experience on the Plantain Islands between 1746 and 1748, when one of his seafaring adventures had gone badly wrong. Luckily for him, his father eventually came to the rescue. The person in

question was John Newton, composer of the even better
known hymn, 'Glorious things of thee are spoken,' and of
numerous others. He was also the instigator of many of William
Cowper's best-loved hymns, such as 'God moves in a mysterious way' and 'O for a closer walk with God'.

With such sensitivity to language, what was it that precluded
Newton from having a similar sensitivity to his fellow human
beings? Why did he find no difficulty in ignoring the lot of
those unfortunate Africans beneath him? Such double standards
were by no means uncommon among Christians of the time.
SPCK, the missionary society, not only owned numerous slaves
in the West Indies, but also its agents saw themselves under no
obligation to transmit the message of the Gospel to those black
slaves. The Evangelical revival, of which Newton was to
become a major part with his ordination in 1764, took a different view, but even so there was no automatic revulsion
against slavery. The Gospel was seen as directed towards our
spiritual condition, not our material. So the sentiments in a
verse from a hymn of the following century ('All things bright
and beautiful') would have fully accorded with Newton's own:
'The rich man in his castle,/ The poor man at his gate./ God
made them high and lowly,/ And ordered their estate.' Providence decreed one's lot in life, and that was that.

Yet it is to John Newton that the person responsible for the
abolition of the slave trade in England turned when he
experienced an Evangelical conversion in 1785. That man was
William Wilberforce. Son of a wealthy merchant from Hull, he
had already entered Parliament at the age of twenty-one, and
was to hold a Yorkshire seat for the next forty-five years (1780–
1825) until ill health forced an early retirement. Yet he was an
unlikely candidate as a social reformer. Of diminutive stature
(he was only five feet tall), he was also shy and, unlike Newton,
came from a privileged background, which might well have
prevented any keen appreciation of social ills. But it was he
who secured through relentless campaigning the abolition of
the slave trade in 1807. He also lived long enough to see the
abolition of the institution itself throughout the British Empire

in 1833, a few days before his own public burial in Westminster Abbey, with Parliament suspended so that all could attend the funeral.

Wilberforce succeeded through a combination of charm, humility and total integrity. Even a rake like the Prince Regent insisted upon the company of this Evangelical night after night in his Brighton home. When the Czar brought some of his Cossacks to London in 1814, it was Wilberforce who put them at their ease by smiling and shaking each of their hands individually. Three years later, when finding a church too packed to enter, instead of using his name to force admittance, in he climbed through a window. Stories like this are legion. It was the total absence of cant and pretence that earned him the unqualified admiration of, among others, his friend the prime minister, Pitt the Younger.

But hard work was also required – petitions and letters galore. To change public opinion, letters went not only all over Britain but also throughout Europe: to Czar Alexander in Russia, to Tallyrand in France, to Marshal Blücher in Prussia, to Pope Pius VII in Rome, and so on. Letters further afield were also not unknown. When the slaves in Haiti revolted and their leader became Emperor Christophe, Wilberforce entered into a regular correspondence with him, particularly on how education might improve the lot of the former slaves that were now his subjects. Wilberforce was alive to the potential propaganda value of erstwhile slaves showing their true potential. Earlier he had done everything in his power to foster the success of the new colony of Sierra Leone, which had been granted to black people who had fought on the British side in the American War of Independence.

Eventually even Newton was persuaded, though some think his conversion to the cause half-hearted. More surprising is Wilberforce's failure to rouse any support from the most influential Evangelical of the day, someone who was a close friend and saintly also in his own way, the Cambridge cleric, Charles Simeon. In all their letters and meetings there is no evidence that Simeon ever came to espouse his friend's passion for the cause. Wilberforce shared Wesley's conviction that slavery was 'that execrable sum of all villainies'. But despite his roots in Wesleyan enthusiasm, Simeon represented that more typical brand of Evangelical, for whom personal holiness was the sum total of the Christian religion. So not for him Wilberforce's social concerns, whether slavery or chimney sweeps. Instead, what attracted him to his friend, apart from his undoubted personal qualities, were such achievements as Wilberforce's role in obtaining free access for missionaries to India or his founding of CMS (the Church Missionary Society). There was also the progress he helped make possible towards the enforcement of Sunday observance.

Simeon himself once confessed: 'I have no imagination – I never had.' That seems confirmed by his description of Cambridge's King's College Chapel to an artist of his day. He chose not to mention any of its artistic glories, but rather its relative size compared to Noah's Ark. Such was his single-minded determination to let the Bible alone be his guide. It is a form of religion with which Wilberforce wrestled long and hard. He was for ever feeling pangs of guilt as his reading in secular literature expanded, particularly through his love of the novels of Sir Walter Scott. In 1807 he had felt compelled to declare that, if abandoned on a desert island, even Shakespeare must be left behind in preference for the moralizing tales of his fellow Evangelical, Hannah Moore, who was then selling in the millions. Wilberforce lived and died an Evangelical. But his later years reveal a mind already searching for something more. Three of his sons he sent not to St. Edmund Hall, the obvious centre in Oxford at that time for Evangelicals, but to Oriel, the college destined to mark the year of his death as the birth of the Oxford or Anglo-Catholic Movement. Again, in a manner very much out of keeping with the times he even entrusted the education of one of his grandchildren to a Roman Catholic tutor. The revolt against Evangelicalism within the Church of England had begun. Archbishop Sumner was to be the last Evangelical Archbishop of Canterbury (he died in 1862) for more than a century until Donald Coggan was appointed in 1974.

The history of the Church of England might have been very different had other Evangelicals shared Wilberforce's imagination and breadth of vision. Yet even Wilberforce failed to see the need for improved workers' rights and so supported the passing of the Combination Act of 1799 that prohibited union activity. Other repressive forms of government control over workers also gained his support, including even the dreadful Peterloo Massacre of 1819 when unarmed civilians were fired on and eleven killed. But before we leap to condemn, recall the situation nearer to our own times, when many sincere Christians in South Africa persuaded themselves of the inherent rightness of apartheid. It is not easy to have a wider vision than the social group with which one commonly associates, still less than that of one's society as a whole.

The problem for the future of Evangelicalism was that it got caught in a rut, with too narrow an understanding of the implications of biblical revelation. Of course, it revived once more, and indeed is now the strongest group generally in Protestant churches, and in the Church of England in particular. But it has changed. Among contemporary Evangelicals social concern is one of the major recurring themes. The movement has learnt the lesson that Wilberforce was striving to apply for his own circle: that personal sanctity is not just a matter of one's own personal relationship with God but equally of how one enables others to relate to God in making possible the full flourishing of their lives, material no less than spiritual. For the two are indissolubly connected, with God creator of one no less than the other. Should that be forgotten, it is not only others who will suffer but us ourselves in our diminished understanding of God and his will for us.

23

Josephine Butler

Caring for those *not* like ourselves

Josephine Butler, as we shall see shortly, is a person of great significance in her own right. But, as has been the norm for most of human history, where she lived and what she experienced were in large part a consequence of her husband's occupation and job moves. So we must begin with him. Josephine Grey came from a distinguished, wealthy and privileged family from the north-east of England, among whom had been numbered a former prime minster, Earl Grey. She first met her future husband, George, at Durham where he was a tutor at University College for a short time until 1850. They married in 1851, with George now teaching at Oxford. Subsequent moves were to take them to Cheltenham and Liverpool, before ill health finally made essential an easier existence for George as a canon of Winchester.

Appalling conditions in the slums of Liverpool were to have a marked impact on Josephine's thinking. But so were intimate contacts through her husband with the clergy of the day. On those in Oxford influenced by the Catholicizing tendencies of the Oxford Movement she is particularly severe: 'There was outward ritual without the inward conviction and fervour which gave it meaning and life in the cradle of its birth.' In general she found 'a conventional mode of looking at things', with those holding different views too 'cautious and timid' to speak out against 'the celibate mass around' – in other words, the unmarried clergy who still dominated Oxford at this time.

Perhaps in reaction, she herself refused to be confined to any particular narrow or sectarian track. Not only does she write a sympathetic account of the medieval saint, Catherine of Siena, she also does not hesitate to criticize Protestant orthodoxy wherever she thought it lacking in sufficient breadth of vision. A case in point is the doctrine of hell as a place of eternal punishment. In her essay, 'The Morning Cometh', she will have none of this and backs up her view with learned and informed accounts of the meaning of the various Greek words in the New Testament. Even so, in her attempt to find in the Bible what she thinks it ought to say, she clearly sometimes oversteps the bounds of probability. So, for instance, she tries to justify Joshua's massacres of the local Canaanite population by suggesting that this way the victims escaped to an easier place of probation in the next life. More plausible is her idea that Paul's acceptance of the inferior status of women should be read as a necessary but temporary accommodation of Christ's teaching to the present state of the world for a faith still struggling to find its foothold within a hostile environment. Such reflection may suggest a woman of limited ability desperately trying to accommodate Scripture to new ideas already current within her society, but in fact in many ways her thinking was well ahead of her time.

The latter remark about Paul occurs in the introduction to a volume of essays which she edited entitled *Woman's Work and Woman's Culture*. Published in 1869, its argument anticipates many of the issues that came to dominate discussion of women's rights in the twentieth century, such as developments in access to education and their property and voting rights. With equally remarkable foresight she argues, by implication, for the ordination of women. So, for instance, in her 1898 essay, 'Prophets and Prophetesses', she observes that the prophecy which was to find its fulfilment in the foundation of the Church at Pentecost (Joel 2.28–9) spoke of 'daughters' and 'handmaids' participating as fully as 'sons' and male 'servants'.

Yet to speak of her as someone ahead of her time really does little to establish what for me marks her true greatness. There was nothing that she wanted for herself. Rather, what motivated her was the conviction that people of her own class and background had failed to observe the appalling consequences which discrimination so often had for women who were poor or working class. So, for instance, she is quick to parody speeches in parliament which opposed public provision of education for girls on the grounds that the proper place for educating them is in the home; she rightly observes that this assumes the upper-class home, with the space and economic resources to accomplish such things.

Such is the wider context against which the campaign for which she is famous should be set, her opposition to the Contagious Diseases Act of 1869, which occupied seventeen years of her life. Napoleon had been the first to experiment with such legislation as a way of protecting his troops from the spread of venereal disease. Various other European countries were to follow suit, and in 1869 Britain did likewise. Local magistrates were given the power to seize women suspected of being prostitutes and to subject them thereafter to a fortnightly examination for up to a year, the penalty for refusal being imprisonment. In effect licensed brothels were being introduced, with women operating near barracks (at home or abroad) particularly subject to regular checks and being moved elsewhere if found to be diseased.

In her desire to show what is wrong with such legislation, Josephine appealed to no less a foundation than the Magna Carta, with its insistence on the avoidance of arbitrary arrest and on equality before the law. For, as she shrewdly observes, for a woman to be condemned under the legislation took the say-so of only one man, and one man at that who was not required to admit any personal culpability or responsibility on his own part. Carefully shielded in effect were all those men who used the services of the prostitutes, while women who were poor, homeless or caught in ambiguous circumstances – for instance, out in a rough area after dark – were now subject to arbitrary arrest.

Josephine was a marvel of organizational ability, travelling throughout western Europe to rally support through conferences and through personal appeal to influential figures. Envoys were also dispatched to the United States to pre-empt the introduction of similar legislation there, something that was already being canvassed, particularly by the medical profession. Inevitably however the brunt of her campaign was within Britain itself. Most of the means she employed, such as public meetings and petitionary letters with hundreds of thousands of signatures, we are equally familiar with today. But she was also successful in unseating MPs, as in the Colchester by-election, where the government Liberal candidate, Sir Henry Storks, lost his seat because of Josephine's campaign against him. This is all the more remarkable in an era when the status of women in public life was still far from secure, with the right to vote several decades off.

All this would be impressive enough, but what makes her for me a truly outstanding spiritual example is the way in which her life and writings again and again reveal a capacity to perceive a situation from a perspective quite different from her own fortunate state. Let me make a personal confession. When in her biography of her husband she tells of the first of the many women they were to take into their home, my first reaction was shock – a child murderer from Newgate, after all. It was only as I read on that I saw the point: the appalling pressures that that woman was under that led her to murder her own child. Again, in her biblical exposition she has an uncanny knack of forcing us to see events from some new angle that can widen our horizons. For example, the woman of Shunem in 2 Kings 4 is taken as the model of an equal marriage. Again, Hagar is made the real hero of the events in Genesis that we normally see as focusing around Abraham and Sarah.

I began with Josephine's critique of the clergy and those of similar social status to herself. What attracted her to Catherine of Siena and led her to write her biography was that she too was faced with similar problems: a weak pope who needed to be needled into doing his duty – moving the papacy back to

Rome from Avignon – and saintly men who used the call of the cloister as an excuse to avoid decisive action in the world, the need to reform the fourteenth-century Church. Despite all the positive indicators of a compassionate Church, is there not today a similar danger of complacency? If I may put it like this, the modern Church is excellent in supporting respectable social concerns such as the fight against poverty and hunger in the developing world. It is less good at supporting unfashionable causes – for example, the integration of the mentally handicapped into the wider society, or challenging a prison system that imposes disproportionate penalties on those of low intelligence and from deprived backgrounds. Josephine Butler displayed no such hesitancy. She identifies with the despised of her day. So did Christ. The challenge remains for us to identify those *unlike* ourselves, alongside whom we should similarly stand.

24

Edith Stein

Beyond guilt and innocence

Events like the September 11th attack on the Twin Towers or, more recently still, the terrorist attack on commuter trains in Madrid early in 2004, when two hundred people were killed and over one thousand injured, cannot help but make us ask: Why does God allow such things? It is a question addressed much less frequently in Scripture than one might have expected. Jesus, however, does respond in a brief exchange recorded in Luke 13.1–9, where he is asked precisely that question in respect of two tragedies from his own day. First, there is the case of some Galileans who had been killed by Pilate while sacrificing (possibly a reference to an incident that eventually led to Pilate's recall). Then there are the eighteen fatalities in Jerusalem itself that occurred when the Tower of Siloam collapsed on them, this time probably the result of some good intentions on the part of Pilate, his attempt to improve the city's water supply with a new aqueduct.

For once, though, Jesus' reply seems strangely inadequate. For, although insisting that the fate of neither group was undeserved – they were no worse or better than anyone else around at the time – he goes on to use the incidents mainly as an excuse for warning of the need for repentance while there is still time. Or at least that was my first impression, but is that right? Might those two elements – the innocence of those who suffer and yet the need to draw some further lesson – be after all precisely what is required in approaching the problem of unmerited suffering? To see why, let us travel back a little in history beyond recent frightening acts of terrorism, and reflect on what happened in the Holocaust.

It is possible of course to look at what happened to the Jews of Europe at this time in quite a number of different ways. For example, the Holocaust is sometimes presented as the inevitable consequence of a long history of Christian anti-Semitism. But there is nothing inevitable about history, and so, awful though the medieval pogroms and ghettoes were, they did not have to lead to the so-called 'final solution'. The real surprise is surely that it happened among one of the most cultured and civilized peoples in Europe. Thereby the death-knoll was sounded for any notion of the inevitability of human progress. The Nazi leaders were by and large thugs, but many ordinary, cultivated Germans were carried along by their propaganda into the conviction that the Jews were responsible for Germany's economic ills and so did deserve expulsion, if not anything worse. The result was that desert and innocence became muddy waters, and with it attitudes to the accompanying suffering. But, Jesus protests, that is the wrong way of looking at things. Suffering is sometimes the outcome of the working of natural laws, sometimes of human evil, but never is it planned by God as punishment.

That is a vitally important response for Christians to hear, because the Bible has no united voice on the subject, and indeed is sometimes found advocating the contrary view. Such a perspective is to be found, for example, in many of the Psalms and historical books of the Old Testament. Indeed, in the case of the author of Chronicles, history is rewritten to make the pattern fit the theology. In order to explain why good King Josiah died at a mere thirty-nine years of age at the Battle of Megiddo, the author invents a divine command that had been disobeyed but that finds no place in the earlier book of Kings (contrast 2 Kgs 23.29–30 and 2 Chron. 35.21–2). The Book of Job was written as a protest against such views, and here Jesus is renewing the protest. Even so, the older theology continued to recur in much subsequent Christian history. Indeed, one has only to think of how some Christians responded to the phenomenon of AIDS to see how hard it is to eradicate such wrong thinking. Sadly, those who protested and spoke of 'victims' were almost as wrongheaded as those who identified the phenomenon as an act of divine justice. To deny divine involvement it was not necessary to claim innocent lives. Guilt and innocence were simply irrelevant. Good and evil alike suffered, and both ought equally to elicit our care and compassion.

This issue is not the one that I want to pursue further here, but rather the more general question of how we should respond personally to suffering when it occurs. Some of us will no doubt live out long lives with little pain in them and much pleasure. Others may be tragically cut short with some devastating illness. Yet others suffer a great deal of mental pain with broken marriages or conflicts with their children. But, however it turns out, in no case has God decreed that particular scenario. Rather, it is simply a matter of the way the general ordering of the world works out in that particular case. Tension, pain and human freedom are all in themselves good things. Tension helps to stimulate and challenge us to action; pain warns us when things are going wrong with our bodies; human freedom makes the direction of our lives largely a matter of our own decisions. But all three can turn against us in the wrong set of circumstances. And then the question becomes not whether we deserved what happens, but rather the extent to which we can then use the result creatively. Just keeping matters on the purely human level for the moment, think of two human beings responding to the same level of physiological pain: arthritis, for example. Their reactions will not necessarily be at all alike. It can lead in the case of one person to his or her early retirement and deep depression, while another will emerge strengthened as a result, now even more determined to achieve certain goals before life reaches its inevitable conclusion in death.

And that is where God comes in, and the second part of Jesus' answer. In his response the two incidents are used as an incentive towards further reflection and repentance, but that is of course by no means the only option. For another, I want to return to the Holocaust, and one saint, canonized as recently as 1998: Edith Stein. She was born in what is now the Polish city of Wroclaw but which was in 1891, the year of her birth, still part of Germany and known as Breslau. She came from a moderately well-to-do Jewish family. Her father, a timber merchant, died when she was only two, and so it was her mother who brought her up. Herself an observant Jew, she did little to encourage the practice of Judaism in any of her seven children. So, perhaps not surprisingly, by the time Edith was an adult she had relinquished any belief she may once have had. Her real passion instead was philosophy, and she studied under one of the great philosophers of the day, Edmund Husserl, himself a major influence on Pope John Paul II's thinking. Husserl had moved from Judaism to Lutheranism. Edith, however, chose Catholicism, and was baptized in her thirties, in 1922. Her real desire was to become a nun, but her advisors urged her to use her great gifts in education, and so entrance to a convent was delayed until 1933, initially at Cologne and then, once war broke out, in Holland at Echt. It was from there that she was deported in 1942 as part of 'the final solution': back once more to Poland, but this time to Auschwitz.

She herself had a great admiration for Teresa of Avila, the sixteenth-century founder of the Discalced Carmelites, and it was this order's founding of a small convent at Auschwitz in Stein's honour that created an international outcry in the mid-1980s. Despite her being Jewish, many Jews felt that having a Christian presence would detract from the uniqueness of the camp's witness to the Holocaust. Eventually, the convent moved off site, but what is really more interesting than the resolution of the conflict is what it tells us, for better or worse, about the two religions' attitude to such suffering. For modern Jews nothing could redeem the past, and so Auschwitz must stand as a permanent warning for Jews to be vigilant in the future, and strong enough to prevent it ever happening again. The positive side has been the creation of the state of Israel; the negative side some of that state's policies, in which the

Palestinians are so often marginalized and badly treated: the Jew no longer always the victim but also sometimes the oppressor.

None of this is intended to minimize the wickedness of Auschwitz, nor to suggest that anything modern Israelis have done, even the notorious 1948 massacre at Deir Yassin, anywhere approaches, even remotely, its moral horrors and debased reality. Nonetheless, one can understand why some Poles were resentful at the compromise positioning of the convent, when one learns that 75,000 non-Jewish Poles and 20,000 gypsies also perished in that same camp. Poles in the past had often been anti-Semitic, but that hardly justified what they suffered in the war, any more than Israel's present policies justifies their casualties in terrorist bombings. The cycle of violence needs to be broken, not perpetuated. Edith Stein herself spoke of offering up her life as a sacrifice on behalf of her people. By that I do not think she meant that she was atoning for their sins. On the contrary, she always remained very proud that she was a Jew. Rather, her point was that she wanted to identify with them in their suffering, despite the fact that she was by religion no longer a Jew. In that way the source of the conflict was transcended, with the most obvious difference in the Jews' religious practice no longer being the key. In a not unrelated way the Polish priest Fr Maksymilian Kolbe sought to make the same affirmation, when he offered his own life in place of a Jewish inmate of the camp.

It is a comfortable delusion to believe in neat categories of innocent and guilty, victim and oppressor. Sometimes of course it is like that, but more commonly human nature reveals a more worrying mix, and it is that mix that we need to face. Christians are sometimes good, sometimes wicked; Jews are sometimes victims, sometimes oppressors. Where Edith Stein achieved her greatness was in refusing classifications. She wanted to identify with all who suffered, Jew or Christian, innocent or guilty. Equally, heaven was not only for those who thought like her, for Edith was confident that there she would find both her Jewish mother (a woman she had not always treated kindly), and Edmund Husserl (a man who had not always treated her

153

kindly). Faults, guilt, suffering were not to have the final say. Through God's gracious help good can come out of evil.

25

Hannington and Luwum

Transcending the colonial past

It was as recently as 1977 that the protests of the Anglican Archbishop of Uganda, Janani Luwum, against the brutal dictatorship of Idi Amin led to his own murder at the hands of the government. Not that he was by any means the first to die in this way. It is estimated that Amin may have killed as many as 300,000 of his fellow nationals. Sadly, there are similar stories of Christian martyrdom to be told, right at the birth of this young nation. Not that such martyrdoms took anything like the same form. The contrast, though, will be interesting to explore in its own right, not least because martyrdom's varying expression can tell us something about not only Africa's growth beyond colonialism but also how, irrespective of context, there is something to be learnt from the widely differing challenges to which Christianity is exposed.

For the earlier martyrdom let us first travel back in time to shortly before the birth of the present nation (effectively a creation of the expanding British empire) to the ancient kingdom of Buganda, on which it was largely based. A few years earlier in 1884 James Hannington had been made Anglican Bishop of Eastern Equatorial Africa, in order to pursue missionary work in the area. Taking a troop of about two hundred natives with him, he sought to forge some new footpaths through the jungle to Lake Victoria. His diaries survive, and it is fascinating to read the combination that we find in him of missionary and explorer. There is not any shadow of doubt in his mind about the superiority of the religion and civilization he is bringing with him, and this appears at times to have given him what can only be described as a foolhardy courage. For instance, his diaries frequently record hostility from the various peoples through whom he passes. Yet, nothing daunted, he nonchalantly strides up to them waving his walking stick in welcome.

Surprisingly, in general his approach seems to have met with remarkable success until his last and fatal encounter, in October 1885. The new, more hostile attitude was initiated by a new king of Buganda, Mwanga, who feared – rightly – that Hannington and his sort would bring British rule in their train. The short-term result was that not only did Hannington perish, but so too did quite a number of the king's entourage, including some quite young boys – some as young as eleven – because of their proven sympathy towards the new faith. At about the same time a number of Roman Catholic missionaries and converts also suffered martyrdom. They were eventually canonized (in 1964). In the third century Tertullian had already spoken of martyrs as the seedbed of the Church. That is precisely what happened in this case also. Only a century later and the majority of the population of Uganda is now Christian.

Not that the history of the intervening century was an unproblematic one. Much of it was characterized by the unhealthy competitive spirit that has so often been displayed in relations between Protestant and Catholic missionaries. Right at the beginning, this is especially prominent in the Protestant group led by a hot-headed Scot, Alexander Mackay, and in the Catholic group led by the French White Father, Simeon Lourdel. Each had as his primary aim the imposition upon all natives of what they themselves saw as the right version of Christianity. It was into such a spirit of fierce competitiveness that Janani Luwum was born in 1922 in northern Uganda. So, not unpredictably, the sort of Protestant Christianity he at first espoused was characterized by strong hostility towards Rome. Equally unsurprising is the fact that the Evangelical faith to which he was first won included stress upon the experience of speaking in tongues and a claimed ability to date conversion to quite specific moments in time. In his case this was set at lunchtime, on 6 January 1948 at 12.30 p.m. exactly.

To some degree those attitudes were reinforced by the period he spent in Britain at the London College of Divinity, but eventually he was to distance himself from such a past to some considerable degree. For if during his time as a bishop in the north of the country he was still fighting with Roman Catholics over how near they should be allowed to build their churches to Anglican schools, by the time he became Arch-bishop of Uganda he had formed a close friendship with his Roman Catholic opposite number. Not only that, although he continued to be suspicious of any version of Christianity that labelled itself liberal, he did come to the conclusion that, however much the liberal, German, New Testament scholar, Rudolf Bultmann (d. 1976) may have been wrong in other ways, he was right in this, the Gospel had to be translated into terms more suited to the contemporary context, and in his case this meant the local African cultural context. So in these and related ways one can see Luwum prior to his death already beginning to transcend the limitations of his own particular background. He already had a shrewd notion of the fruitful direction in which he might have led his church, had he been granted longer life.

But Idi Amin put an end to all that. During his reign of terror that lasted from 1971 to 1979, Amin was to rely heavily on the support of Islamic governments such as those of Colonel Gadaffi of Libya, and he himself became a Muslim. While it would be absurd to speak of Amin's rule as having any kind of legitimacy, that conversion does, I think, highlight one perti-nent issue for our own day: Amin thought he was pursuing a more African course, free of the shackles of the country's British imperial past.

Much further south, a similar policy of disengagement was adopted by a quite different person, Steve Biko, one of the heroes of the anti-apartheid movement. Eventually murdered in that same fateful year by the white government there, he was made the subject of a powerful film by Richard Attenborough, *Cry Freedom*. For Biko the Christianity of his youth suggested too close an association with the types of attitudes and assumptions that had led to apartheid in the first place. Biko and Amin, hugely different though they were, alike represent a common response in our modern world, the attempt to escape our 'conditionedness' by resorting to some quite different ordering of reality. But does it work? Or is it not the case that new forms of conditioning emerge, and sometimes they are even more devastating than what they are supposed to supplant, as with Idi Amin? Might there not be some better way, where the burden of the past is fully acknowledged, yet not allowed the final say?

Consider once more the two martyrs whose lives we have been examining. Both were good and courageous men. Both were also creatures of a particular time and a particular place. Hannington displayed many of the attitudes characteristic of a British patriot of the time. Indeed, his obvious delight in shooting game or in eating monkey reads almost like a self-parody. Similarly, Luwum was – conspicuously – the product of a very specific type of conservative, anti-Catholic, Evangelical upbringing. In describing them as holy men we must not therefore suppose that we are committed to endorsing every aspect of their lives and attitudes. Equally, however, we must avoid despising those specific contexts, for we are no less products of a particular time and culture. Their strength lay in the degree to which, while remaining within those limitations, they also transcended them, and I want to end by noting how they did so. For, if we are really willing to allow their limitations to cast light on our own, we may yet learn from them, no less from where they were limited than from where their values appear more universal.

Take Hannington first. It is of course much easier for us, more than a century later, to see all the negative aspects and ambiguities inherent in colonialism and its inheritance. Even so, Hannington never became the sort of English patriot who despised the African. Rather, it was precisely because he valued the native peoples that he wanted to convert them. In our own day colonialism is no longer an issue, but attitudes to immigrants and asylum seekers certainly are. It is disconcerting to learn that the number of the latter welcomed into Britain in recent years is significantly lower than that to many another European country, including Germany. Jingoism is not a fault that ceased with the nineteenth century. Whereas nationalism went with generosity of spirit in the case of Hannington, it is doubtful whether the same can really be said of a nation like contemporary Britain, where the popular press frequently plays on our suspicions of those of different colour or race, and regularly pretends to possess an innate moral superiority to our cousins in continental Europe.

Again, Luwum might so easily have continued the acute suspicion of Roman Catholics among Protestants with which his nation began, in the work of Alexander Mackay and others. To his credit, he did not. Modern Britain scarcely exhibits parallel tensions, but in the context of 'the war against terrorism' there are similarities in unreasoned suspicions against Muslims. Too often in modern society an easy superiority to other cultures and creeds is simply assumed, and so we disguise from ourselves how shallow contemporary English society in fact is. We desperately need the past to throw fresh light on our own present. For all the limitations of their background, Hannington and Luwum at least refused to let those limitations have total control over their perspective. Where they saw conflict with the underlying message of the Christian faith, they faced it out. So too must we in our own quite different context, and there is no doubt that studying lives of such holy people from the past can help us in that task.

Conclusion

26

Heaven alongside

Interceding saints

In the preceding pages I have tried to bring sanctity alive by suggesting that those we call saints are neither carbon copies of one another nor merely straightforward attempts at imitating Christ. Rather, each brings his or her own distinctive contribution to the age in which they happen to find themselves, as well as exposing the limitations that specific cultural contexts inevitably also entail. Exploring just how that more complex form of mediating Christ's example works is itself a challenging and rewarding task. But this by no means exhausts the relevance of such people to our own lives. So I want to conclude this book with some further discussion of where I believe the saints now to be, and why their presence in the heaven so described might be of special relevance to our own practice of the Christian faith. To do so I would like to approach the issue by three stages: first, by raising the question of location; then, second, of content, whether traditional representations do not make heaven seem fundamentally boring and unattractive; and finally, and most pertinent to the topic of this book, of the issue of interaction, how the saints might actually impinge on our own lives in the here and now.

On the question of location, I suspect that the starting point for most people, even for most Christians, is a sense of the great distance between heaven and ourselves. The Bible is full of images of the transcendence of God, in terms of which his essential presence lies elsewhere (e.g. Isa. 66.1; Ps. 115.16). Certainly, there is another side. In the Old Testament the Temple is regarded as a special focus of divine presence, and numerous features of the natural world (mountains, trees, burning bush, and so on) are employed to evoke a sense of at least an episodic divine immanence. That sense of presence within our own world then becomes more focused in the New, both with the incarnation and the way in which the activity of the Holy Spirit is conceived. Nonetheless, it is often the images of distance and otherness that continue to exercise the most influence. So we need to face head on what these might entail. No doubt some of the biblical writers did take literally the notion of God's normal residence being up there in the heavens. But, however disposed in that direction they may have been, they could not but also have been aware of the symbolic content that runs deep within such language, the way in which it draws attention to the contrast with humanity and thus the resultant need for awe before the divine majesty. Indeed, the fact that in so many languages the word for 'heaven' and for 'God' share the same root confirms, I suggest, that rather more was involved than simply the question of divine location even for the most 'primitive' of peoples. The height of the heavens was taken to provide a fundamental clue to the reality of what it is to be divine: as exalted and as far above ordinary humanity as the heavenly vault appears to be above our eyes.

God is by definition in any case present everywhere ('omnipresent'). So there can be no doubt that 'up there' is quite the wrong language to employ, if one intends to go beyond employment of such a powerful spatial metaphor for something else (God's character) into actual description of the divine mode of existence. Nearness and awe are in fact quite compatible, and so a less misleading form of imagery needs to be found. For one possibility let me take readers back to their childhood, and a book of relevance not only to children: C. S. Lewis' *The Lion, the Witch and the Wardrobe*. The wardrobe was for the children in the story the point of transition between this world and another, more exciting reality. Yet in moving back and forth between the two worlds, both time and space stood still. There was no 'up there', nor a time that could have an impact on our own. Instead, the two worlds touched, without one altering the fundamental character of the other. To my mind heaven has always seemed something like that, a near but independent world that compels us to acknowledge otherness but in a way that does not bounce it off the horizon of our consciousness.

Although not talking explicitly of the saints in heaven, Augustine of Hippo put the point well. God's heaven is all around us rather like the water in a sponge: the divine presence (and so presumably also that of heaven itself) permeates the sponge of our world in such a way that nowhere on earth is farther apart from God's world than any other. The nineteenth-century poet Francis Thompson is presumably drawing on a similar line of thought when in a well-known poem he speaks of Jacob's ladder 'pitched betwixt Heaven and Charing Cross' and of 'Christ walking on the water/ Not of Gennesareth, but Thames'.[36] The image is of angels drawing the two worlds close, a theme taken up by Newman in one of his sermons when he suggests: 'Every breath of air and ray of light and heat, every beautiful prospect is, as it were, the skirts of their garments, the waving of the robes of those whose faces see God in heaven.'[37]

Both Thompson and Newman are essentially nineteenth-century figures. Despite all the uncertainties of that particular age, there was in general a liveliness about Victorian belief in the after-life that is now sadly lacking. Consider a mid-century response to suffering and mortality. In the 1850s a future Archbishop of Canterbury (who was at that time Dean of Carlisle) lost six of his eight young children in one fell swoop as the result of an outbreak of scarlet fever. As the tragedy struck home, the response turned out very differently from what we might expect today, even from a Christian. Mrs Tait, his wife, describes how all her young children ask eagerly whether they will soon be joining their Saviour in heaven, while one of them even goes so far as to dress up as a angel by way of preparation.

Meanwhile her husband wrote in his diary: 'Though thou slay us, Lord, yet will we trust in thee . . . They are gone from us, all but Craufurd and the babe. Thou hast reclaimed the lent jewels. Yet, O Lord, shall I not thank thee now? . . . I thank thee for the blessings of the last ten years, and for all the sweet memories of their little lives . . . I thank thee for the bright hopes of a happy reunion, when we shall meet to part no more.'[38] Despite the enormous extent of the tragedy, there is a confidence, a certainty here that much contemporary Christianity lacks.

In contributing to such changed attitudes, no doubt many factors have played their part. Here I want to address only one that is relevant to our theme, the issue of content: why for so many today the whole notion of heaven sounds inherently boring and unattractive. Janáček's opera, *The Makropoulos Case*, may be used to illustrate the point. The plot concerns a certain Elina Makropoulos, who each year in order to avoid death has been taking a magical elixir of life that permanently preserves her at age forty-two, though her real age is now three hundred and forty-two years. Her unending life, however, has come to be for her a state of boredom, indifference and coldness. 'In the end,' she says, 'it is the same, singing and silence.' So this time she refuses the elixir, and dies. In the opera the action is set on earth, but we might say the same conclusion applies equally to Christian descriptions of heaven. Even the most devoted of choirs might get a little bored with the endless anthems to God that St John the Divine envisages in the Book of Revelation.

So, what about this for an alternative description? 'When the earth shakes and quivers, and the mountains crumble and scatter abroad into fine dust, you shall be divided. Those on the right hand shall be brought near to their Lord in the gardens of delight . . . They shall recline on jewelled couches face to face and there shall wait on them immortal youths with bowls and ewers and a cup of finest wine' – and here comes a nice touch – 'wine that will neither pain their heads nor take away their reason; [waited on] with fruits of their own choice and flesh of fowls that they relish. And theirs shall be the dark eyed virgins, chaste as hidden pearls, a guerdon for their deeds . . . They shall recline ... amidst gushing waters and abundant fruits, unforbidden, never-ending.'[39]

That is the description we are offered in the Qur'an. Things, however, are seldom quite as they appear. Mohammad forbade both the taking of alcohol and promiscuity; so, whatever he meant, he cannot have intended that we take the images literally. And that point is as true of the images in the Book of Revelation. What is being hinted at is a new status, a new relationship, quite beyond any adequate imagining on our part. Mohammad deliberately chose images that would appeal to the common man, not because he thought that heaven would really be like that, but because he recognized the most basic fact about its reality: that it would fulfil every desire of who we will *then* be in reality, even if now lust and booze are what give us our present identity.

So similarly then with the images of Revelation. The endless exploration of the infinite riches of God could not possibly be boring for someone who truly loves God, nor could the indefinite extension of one's friendships to all the myriads from past, present and future who now share God's presence. Of course, it would be infinitely boring if one refuses that identity beyond self that is love, but then heaven is not for us as we are, but as we might be, through God's grace.

But that is still not yet to give the whole answer. In my second introductory chapter I indicated how Christ was dependent on others during his earthly life and continued in dependence on the saints thereafter, in that they now mediate how Christ's example might be lived out in what are often quite different circumstances. There is, however, another aspect of dependence for Christ which I have not as yet addressed, and that is a dependence on other human beings even in heaven itself. To some this may sound almost blasphemous, but the point is that the doctrine of the ascension asserts not simply the presence of Christ's divinity in heaven but also the continuing identity of his whole humanity there as well. Many (pagan and Christian alike) would acknowledge that a key aspect of what it is to be human is to be a social being, that one lives at least in part through others and indeed largely acquires one's particular sense of identity through one's relationship with other human beings. But if that is so, then surely this must apply no less to Jesus in heaven as perfect representative of our own humanity than it does to the rest of us. It seems, therefore, that true humanity is not there, unless heaven is, as it were, populated, not just by Christ but by at least some fellow human beings.

This is a point of no small moment, for, as we shall see, it affects not only the quality of life in heaven but also its potential impact on us. In protesting against some being exalted over others as 'saints', it is very easy to move to the conclusion that all distinctions are therefore abolished, a world in which only one uniform kind of perfection exists. For some, like Tom Wright, it may be welcome as suggesting a radical egalitarianism, but of course fresh problems come in their turn. Can God, for example, really be said to respect our individuality if our personalities change in a flash without our ever comprehending or being asked to endorse that change? Purgatory as a place of purgation (not punishment) at least acknowledges the gradualism needed to appropriate such changes as our very own, necessitated as they are by the true estimate of our characters that we now have. It also means that each change carries its own distinctive story, with each transformation of character unique to that particular individual.

Equally, however, there are problems for the nature of heaven if we are all now supposed to be fundamentally alike. For wherein then lies the interest in getting to know each other better? Take Christ himself. Certainly he is no longer in pain, but that surely does not mean that unpleasant memories from the past do not continue to shape the kind of person he now is. His attitude to close and intimate relationships, for example, cannot but have been affected by what Judas did to him, by the numerous other ways in which his disciples let him down, and by the memory of his distrustful brothers who thought him a madman and only came to faith after his death. Equally, for the apostle Peter an indispensable element in his identity must continue to be the fact that he denied his Lord. So their relation in heaven cannot be about forgetting that this ever happened, but about its significance being transformed through Christ's forgiveness. Each of heaven's inhabitants will thus have a form of perfection unique to his or her self, a history of faults and their correction that contributes to making them the kind of distinctive individuals that they now are.

This matters because it offers humanity a variety of means for negotiating the whole gamut of sin and failure in our own experience. There is a marvellous passage in a prayer of Anselm's to Mary Magdalene that runs as follows: 'Recall in loving kindness what you used to be, how much you needed mercy, and seek for me that same forgiving love that you received when you were wanting it . . . Draw me to him where I may wash away my sins; bring me to him who can slake my thirst; pour over me those waters that will make my dry places fresh. You will not find it hard to gain all you desire from so loving and so kind a Lord, who is alive and reigns and is your friend'.[40] Forget the fact that the historical figure was almost certainly not the prostitute Anselm implies. The point is that we find it easier to get beyond our faults if we know of someone who has experienced similar difficulties, and yet achieved intimacy with Christ despite them. Just think, for instance, how often people seek out as a confessor or spiritual director someone whom they believe to have once had very similar faults to themselves; or again of how we particularly value the prayers of someone who has had to go through a similar crisis, such as a serious illness or a difficult job move. But if that is a powerful stimulus towards appealing for the prayers of one living contemporary rather than another, why should it not be also in choosing among those who have passed beyond the grave?

For some, to talk in this way may be already to detract from the unique role of Christ. But the objection, I think, misses the point. It is not that the saints then of themselves do something directly, any more than this would be true of an intercessor still living here on this earth. Indeed, in some ways there is less risk of sidestepping Christ in appealing to the dead for help, for in their case whether the request is ever heard by them is presumably itself in the hands of God, whereas the earthly intercessor can still be approached directly. The purpose is thus not to bypass Christ but to seek Christ's aid through the type of identity he himself came to give us, as part of his one body which is the Church, a social community that transcends the particular time and place that happens to be our own lot.

Inevitably, because Christ's early disciples still believed that the world would soon end, the dominant image in the New Testament is of resurrection for all at the end of time in a new world (e.g. 1 Cor. 7.29). As that hope receded, the Church began to make more of the minority position that is also to be found there, of heaven as some sort of waiting place (Lk. 23.43; 2 Cor. 12.2; Phil. 1.23). Yet that it must also be more than just waiting becomes clear as soon as we reflect on Christ's own present position. For, if Christ's complete humanity is now in heaven (as orthodoxy requires), then, whatever is meant by his resurrection from the dead, it cannot be just crudely physical or exclusively tied to this world. There must, in short, be other ways of being completely human than being tied to the material reality of this world (cf. 2 Cor. 5.1–3). Scientific talk of parallel universes may be of some small help here, in its descriptions of other worlds alongside our own but yet quite different. And what holds true of Christ must hold equally for the rest of humanity because, as Scripture repeatedly affirms, he is the first fruits of the dead, not an isolated exception (e.g. 1 Cor. 15.20). So it makes sense to think of the saints in heaven enjoying a similar form of reality to Christ's: full, yet not material at least in the way this world is. This then is what makes possible their participation in our own life: God mediating to them some understanding of how individuals with similar histories are now faring.

Of course, as we have seen, who has been canonized and who not has been a somewhat arbitrary exercise, to say the least. The lists are there only as rough guides as to whom it might be appropriate to evoke. But that said, one's breadth of vision, one's sense of being part of some very much larger enterprise will be considerably enhanced if common interest, fault or place are allowed to encourage active engagement with some of that great heavenly company, meditating on their lives and seeking their prayers.

One last thought. Such a rich life for the saints in heaven may seem to entail that any notion of a future bodily resurrection can therefore now be discounted. It does not. We can continue to hope for a more complete redemption of the world that includes not just the human race but all that God has created. In holding that hope, however, our confidence can be immeasurably strengthened by the realization that it is not simply Christ who is working alongside us, or even all our fellow Christians here on earth, but also that great host beyond the grave willing us on to our shared future. 'Turn but a stone and start a wing,' advises Thompson in his poem, urging us, like the Epistle to the Hebrews, to expect to entertain angels unawares (Heb. 13.2). But more exciting by far in my view is to hear the gentle rustle of the thin veil that separates this world from heaven so nearby, and through the rustle Hebrews' 'great cloud of witnesses' (Heb. 12.1), infinite in its variety yet united in its mediation of Christ.

Notes

1 In chapter 2 of my *Discipleship and Imagination* (Oxford: Oxford University Press, 2000), 62–101, esp. 66–79.

2 As in his splendid black chalk drawing in the Royal Collection. Illustrated in J. Roberts (ed.), *A Millennium Celebration* (London: Royal Collection, 2000), 40–1.

3 N. T. Wright, *The Resurrection of the Son of God* (London: SPCK, 2003).

4 Still in place in Chiesa dei Santi Nazaro e Celso, Brescia. For an illustration, see F. Vacanover *et al.*, *Titian: Prince of Painters* (New York: Prestel, 1990), 88.

5 N. T. Wright, *For All The Saints?* (London: SPCK, 2003).

6 For a good scrubbing, 5; for friends at the palace, 3, 16.

7 M. Staniforth (trans.), *Early Christian Writings* (Harmondsworth: Penguin, 1987), 125.

8 A. Oden (ed.), *In Her Words: Women's Writings in the History of Christian Thought* (Nashville: Abingdon, 1994), 37.

9 J. de Voragine, *The Golden Legend* (Princeton: Princeton University Press, 1993), II, 343.

10 I am summarizing 1.5 of his text here. For Jesus' baptism, see 2.5–6 of Hilary's commentary, most easily available in a French edition: J. Doignon (ed.), *Sur Matthieu* (Paris: Editions du Cerf, 1978).

11 Bede, *A History of the English Church and People* (London: Penguin, 1986), 66 (I, 23).

12 E. Gibbon, *Decline and Fall of the Roman Empire*, ch. XLV (London: Everyman, 1994), 4. 529.

13 Quoted in G. R. Evans, *The Thought of Gregory the Great* (Cambridge: Cambridge University Press, 1986), 19.

14 *Gospel Homily*, X.

15 *Epistle* XI to Mellitus.

16 For a brief summary of opposing evaluations of her significance, see D. Baker, 'A Nursery of Saints: St Margaret of Scotland reconsidered' in D. Baker (ed.), *Medieval Women* (Oxford: Blackwell, 1978), 119–41.

17 *Epistle* 120. Quoted and discussed in R. W. Southern, *Saint Anselm: A Portrait in a Landscape* (Cambridge: Cambridge University Press, 1990), 148–65, esp. 155.

18 R. W. Church, *Life of St Anselm* (London: Macmillan, 1870), 223.

19 *Proslogion*, chs 16 and 26; my trans.

20 *Letter* 190; *Treatise on the Errors of Abelard*.

21 *On Grades of Humility*, ch. 10.

22 *On Loving God*, chs 1–5.

23 *On the Steps of Humility*, ch. 3.

24 Verse 3 of J. M. Neale's translation: *New English Hymnal*, no. 432. 'Jerusalem the Golden' (no. 381) also employs a Neale translation.

25 Letter of August, 1379: K. Foster and M. J. Ronayne (eds.), *I Catherine: Select Writings of Catherine of Siena* (London: Collins, 1980), 257. The next two quotations (from letters to Hawkwood and to Pope Gregory) are from the same book, 69 and 123. The letter to Pope Gregory is from June or July 1376.

26 Catherine of Siena, *The Dialogue* (London: SPCK, Classics of Western Spirituality series, 1980), 27. For God drunk with love, 55; for the image of the bridge, 58 and 64ff. The final quotation is a more literal rendering of some words on p. 58.

27 Not surprisingly, the first comes from an opponent (Thomas Gascoigne), the second from a friend (Adam Usk).

28 The discussion 'On the retirement of Charles V' is reproduced in A. M. Williams (ed.), *Conversations at Little Gidding* (Cambridge: Cambridge University Press, 1970).

29 'Little Gidding' III, esp. lines 14–17.

30 Her own description of the experience is given in her autobiography: *Life*, ch. 29.

31 *Interior Castle*, ch. 2.

32 *Interior Castle* 7, 4.

33 The attribution is made in a number of collections of prayers, but like St Francis' famous prayer it seems more to express similar sentiments than to be derived from her actual words.

34 The correspondence is quoted in A. Dallimore, *Susanna* (Darlington: Evangelical Press, 1992), 162–4.

35 See A. J. Lewis, *Zinzendorf: The Ecumenical Pioneer* (Philadelphia: Westminster Press, 1962).

36 From the penultimate and last verse of the poem that begins: 'O world invisible, we view thee'.

37 *Parochial and Plain Sermons*, II, 29.

38 Quoted from Tait's diaries (for 1856) in R. T. Davidson and W. Benham, *Life of Archibald Campbell Tait* (London: Macmillan, 1891), I, 190.

39 Qur'an, LVI, 12–23: trans. N. J. Dawood, *The Koran* (Harmondsworth: Penguin, 1966), 108–9.

40 B. Ward (trans.), *The Prayers and Meditations of Saint Anselm* (London: Penguin, 1973), 202.

Appendix: Dates

(Including, where appropriate, their feast-days in the Anglican and/or Roman Catholic liturgical calendars.)

Abelard	1079–1142	
Aidan	d. 651	August 31st
Ambrose	339–97	December 7th
Anselm	1033–1109	April 21st
Antony of Egypt	d. 356	January 17th
Arundel, Thomas	1352–1414	
Athanasius	296–373	May 2nd
Augustine of Canterbury	d. between 604–9	May 26th
Becket, Thomas	1120–70	December 29th
Bernard of Clairvaux	1090–1153	August 20th
Butler, Joseph	1692–1752	June 16th
Butler, Josephine	1828–1906	May 30th
Catherine of Siena	1347–80	April 29th
Charles V	1500–58	
Chrysostom	347–407	September 13th
Columba	521–97	June 9th
Cosin, John	1594–1672	
Cranmer, Thomas	1489–1556	March 21st
Ferrar, Nicholas	1592–1637	December 4th

Gregory the Great	540–604	September 3rd
Hannington, James	1847–85	October 29th
Hilary	315–67	January 13th
Hildebrand	d. 1085 (Pope Gregory VII from 1073)	
Luwum	1922–77	February 17th
Margaret of Scotland	1046–93	November 16th
Newton, John	1725–1807	
Perpetua	d. 203	March 7th
Polycarp	69–155	February 23rd
Simeon	1759–1836	November 13th
Stein, Edith	1891–1942	August 9th
Teresa of Avila	1515–82	October 15th
Wesley, John	1703–91	May 24th
Wilberforce, William	1759–1833	July 30th

Further Reading

Abelard: M. T. Clancy, *Abelard: A Medieval Life* (Oxford: Blackwell, 1997); B. Radice (trans.), *Letters of Abelard* (Harmondsworth: Penguin, rev. edn., 2003)

Aidan: Bede, *A History of the English Church and People* (London: Penguin, 1968), 144–5, 163–70; S. Baring-Gould, *Lives of the Northumbrian Saints* (Llanerch: Llanerch Enterprises, 1990), 17–25

Ambrose: B. Ramsey, *Ambrose* (London: Routledge, 1997); J. Moorhead, *Ambrose: Church and Society in the Late Roman World* (London: Longman, 1999)

Anselm: B. Ward (trans.), *The Prayers and Meditations of Saint Anselm* (London: Penguin, 1973); R. W. Southern, *Saint Anselm: Portrait in a Landscape* (Cambridge: Cambridge University Press, 1990)

Antony of Egypt: Athanasius, *The Life of Antony* in 'Classics of Western Spirituality' series (London: SPCK, 1980); D. J. Chitty (trans.), *The Letters of Saint Antony the Great* (Oxford: Fairacres Publications, 1975)

Arundel, Thomas: M. Aston, *Thomas Arundel* (Oxford: Clarendon Press, 1967)

Athanasius: G. L. Prestige, *Fathers and Heretics* (London:

SPCK, 1968), ch. 4; A. Pettersen, *Athanasius* (London: Chapman, 1995)

Augustine of Canterbury: M. Deansley, *Augustine of Canterbury* (London: Nelson, 1964)

Becket, Thomas: T. S. Eliot, *Murder in the Cathedral* (London: Faber, 1938); F. Barlow, *Thomas Becket* (London: Phoenix Press, 2000)

Bernard of Clairvaux: G. Evans (trans.), *Bernard of Clairvaux: Selected Works* (New York: Paulist Press, 1987); E. Gilson, *The Mystical Theology of St Bernard* (Kalamazoo, Michigan: Cistercian Publications, 1990); B. T. McGuire, *The Difficult Saint: Bernard of Clairvaux and his Tradition* (Kalamazoo, Michigan: Cistercian Publications, 1991)

Butler, Joseph: W. A. Spooner, *Bishop Butler* (London: Methuen, 1901); J. Butler, *The Analogy of Religion* (New York: Ungar, 1961)

Butler, Josephine: E. M. Bell, *Josephine Butler: Flame of Fire* (London: Constable, 1962); A. Loades, *Feminist Theology: Voices from the Past* (Oxford: Polity, 2001), 73–139

Catherine of Siena: S. Noffke (trans.), *The Dialogue* in 'Classics of Western Spirituality' series (London: SPCK, 1980); K. Foster and M. J. Ronayne (eds), *I Catherine: Selected Writings of Catherine of Siena* (London: Collins, 1980)

Charles V: M. F. Alvarez, *Charles V* (London: Thames and Hudson, 1975); W. Stirling, *The Cloister Life of the Emperor Charles V* (London: Parker, 1853)

Chrysostom: J. N. D. Kelly, *Golden Mouth: The Story of John Chrysostom* (Grand Rapids, Michigan: Baker Books, 1995); W. Mayer, *John Chrysostom* (London: Routledge, 2000)

Columba: I. Finlay, *Columba* (Edinburgh: Chambers, 1992); R. Sharpe (trans.), *Adomnan's Life of St Columba* (Harmondsworth: Penguin, 1995)

Cosin, John: R. H. Osmond, *A Life of John Cosin* (London: Mowbray, 1913); 'Peter Smart' in G. W. Kitchin, *Seven Sages of Durham* (London: Unwin, 1911); Appendix A in *Durham High Commission Court* (*Surtees Society*, Vol. 34, 1858)

Cranmer, Thomas: R. Lacey *The Life and Times of Henry VIII* (London: Weidenfeld and Nicholson, 1972); D. McCullough, *Thomas Cranmer* (New Haven: Yale University Press, 1996); J. Ridley, *Thomas Cranmer* (Oxford: Clarendon Press, 1962)

Ferrar, Nicholas: A. L. Maycock, *Nicholas Ferrar of Little Gidding* (London: SPCK, 1938); A. M. Williams (ed.), *Conversations at Little Gidding* (Cambridge: Cambridge University Press, 1970)

Gregory the Great: R. A. Markus, *Gregory the Great and his World* (Cambridge: Cambridge University Press, 1997); C. Straw, *Gregory the Great: Perfection in Imperfection* (Berkeley: University of California Press, 1988)

Hannington, James: *The Last Journals of James Hannington* (London: Seeley & Co., 1888)

Hilary: S. McKenna (trans.), *The Trinity* (New York: Fathers of the Church, 1954)

Hildebrand: A. J. Macdonald, *Hildebrand: A Life of Gregory VII* (London: Methuen, 1932); H. E. J. Cowdrey, *Pope Gregory VII* (Oxford: Clarendon Press, 1998)

Luwum: Susan Bergman, *Cloud of Witnesses: 20th Century Martyrs* (London: HarperCollins, 1997); Margaret Ford, *Janani: The Making of a Martyr* (London: Marshall, Morgan and Scott, 1978)

Margaret of Scotland: A. J. Wilson, *St Margaret of Scotland* (Edinburgh: John Donald, 1993); Prior Turgot, trans. I. MacDonald, *Saint Margaret* (Edinburgh: Floris, 1993)

Newton, John: B. Martin, *John Newton and the Slave Trade* (London: Longman, 1961); D. B. Hindmarsh, *John Newton and* *the English Evangelical Tradition* (Grand Rapids, Michigan: Eerdmans, 2001)

Perpetua: 'The Martyrdom of Perpetua' in A. Oden (ed.), *In Her Own Words* (Nashville: Abingdon Press, 1994), pp. 26–37

Polycarp: 'The Martyrdom of Polycarp' in A. Louth and M. Staniforth (eds) *Early Christian Writings* (London: Penguin, 1987), pp. 125–35.

Simeon, Charles: H. E. Hopkins, *Charles Simeon of Cambridge* (London: Hodder and Stoughton, 1977)

Stein, Edith: P. Lyne, *Edith Stein Discovered: A Personal Portrait* (Leominster: Gracewing, 2000); S. Borden, *Edith Stein* (London: Continuum, 2004)

Teresa of Avila: J. M. Cohen (trans.), *The Life of Teresa by Herself* (London: Penguin, 1987); S. Clissold, *Teresa of Avila* (London: Sheldon Press, 1979); R. Williams, *Teresa of Avila* (London: Geoffrey Chapman, 1991)

Wesley, John: H. D. Rack, *Reasonable Enthusiast: John Wesley and the Rise of Methodism* (London: Epworth Press, 1989); A. Dallimore, *Susanna* (Darlington: Evangelical Press, 1992); A. C. Outler and R. P. Heitzenrater (eds), *John Wesley's Sermons: An Anthology* (Nashville: Abingdon, 1984); P. C. Erb (ed.), *Pietists: Selected Writings* (London: SPCK, 1983), pp. 289–330 (for some of Zinzendorf's writings)

Wilberforce, William: O. Warner, *William Wilberforce and his Times* (London: Batsford, 1962); R. Furneaux, *William Wilberforce* (London: Hamilton, 1974)

Index